Fabricating Authenticity

Working with Culture on the Edge
Edited by Vaia Touna, University of Alabama

This series of small books draws on revised versions of posts that originally appeared online at edge.ua.edu—the blog for *Culture on the Edge*, a research collaborative engaged in rethinking identity studies. Each chapter is complemented by an original response from an early career scholar outside the group, that presses the chapter in new directions, either by applying its approach to novel situations or by offering a critique that enhances the approach. Each volume in the series therefore demonstrates how to work with a more dynamic, historically-sensitive approach to identity, as exemplified at a host of ordinary social sites – on varied themes, from museums and popular music to ordering at fast-food restaurants. The brief chapters retain the informality of blogging, modeling for readers how scholars can better examine the contingent and therefore changeable practices that help to create the conditions in which we claim to be an enduring something.

Each volume opens with a brief general Introduction to the key word on which it focuses and ends with an Afterword that tackles wider issues of relevance to the volume's main theme.

Ideal for a variety of classes in which identity or the past are discussed, these small books can either set the table for more in-depth readings in a course or be paired with their suggested resources to comprise an entire course's readings. Thoroughly collaborative, cross-disciplinary, and cross-generational in nature, *Working with Culture on the Edge* provides an opportunity to rethink identity with a group of scholars committed to pressing identity studies in new directions.

Published

Fabricating Difference
Edited by Steven W. Ramey

Fabricating Identities
Edited by Russell. T. McCutcheon

Fabricating Origins
Edited by Russell T. McCutcheon

Fabricating Authenticity

Edited by
Jason W. M. Ellsworth and Andie Alexander

SHEFFIELD UK   BRISTOL CT

Published by Equinox Publishing Ltd.

UK: Office 415, The Workstation, 15 Paternoster Row, Sheffield, South Yorkshire S1 2BX

USA: ISD, 70 Enterprise Drive, Bristol, CT 06010

www.equinoxpub.com

First published 2024

© Jason W. M. Ellsworth, Andie Alexander, and contributors 2024

All rights reserved. No part of this publication may be reproduced or transmitted in any form or by any means, electronic or mechanical, including photocopying, recording or any information storage or retrieval system, without prior permission in writing from the publishers.

British Library Cataloguing-in-Publication Data
A catalogue record for this book is available from the British Library.

ISBN-13 978 1 80050 144 7 (hardback)
          978 1 80050 145 4 (paperback)
          978 1 80050 146 1 (ePDF)
          978 1 80050 587 2 (ePub)

Library of Congress Cataloging-in-Publication Data
Names: Ellsworth, Jason W. M., editor. | Alexander, Andie, editor.
Title: Fabricating authenticity / edited by Jason W. M. Ellsworth and Andie Alexander.
Description: Sheffield, South Yorkshire ; Bristol, CT : Equinox Publishing Ltd, 2024. | Series: Working with Culture on the edge ; vol. 4 | Includes bibliographical references and index. | Summary: "Fabricating Authenticity explores everyday examples that work as productive conversation-starters for those wanting to complicate and examine authenticity claims, thus making this an ideal volume for the introductory classroom and beyond"-- Provided by publisher.
Identifiers: LCCN 2024013396 (print) | LCCN 2024013397 (ebook) | ISBN 9781800501447 (hardback) | ISBN 9781800501454 (paperback) | ISBN 9781800501461 (pdf) | ISBN 9781800505872 (epub)
Subjects: LCSH: Authenticity (Philosophy) | Group identity. | Social groups.
Classification: LCC B105.A8 F33 2024 (print) | LCC B105.A8 (ebook) | DDC 128--dc23/eng/20240508
LC record available at https://lccn.loc.gov/2024013396
LC ebook record available at https://lccn.loc.gov/2024013397

Typeset by S.J.I. Services, New Delhi

Contents

Preface		ix
Introduction: Commodifying Authenticity		1
Jason W. M. Ellsworth and Andie Alexander		
1.	Is There Lettuce in a Greek Salad?	16
	Russell T. McCutcheon	
2.	Beyond Authenticity?	24
	Ian Alexander Cuthbertson	
3.	Marketing the Authentic Taco	30
	Jason W. M. Ellsworth	
4.	A Remembrance of Dishes Past	34
	Rachel D. Brown	
5.	Because YOU'RE an Early Adopter (and I'M NOT): Commodity Fetishism and Identification	39
	Christopher R. Cotter	
6.	Fool's Gold: Tapping into Luxury	45
	Ping-hsiu Alice Lin	
7.	"Maybe she's born with it. Maybe it's Maybelline."	51
	Tara Baldrick-Morrone	
8.	Satisfaction Not Guaranteed: COVID-19, Higher Ed, and the Politics of "Experience"	54
	Sierra L. Lawson	
9.	A Man, A Tan, "God's Plan"	59
	Richard Newton	

vi   *Fabricating Authenticity*

10. Just in It for a Paycheck?: On Philanthrocapitalism,
    Petro-States, and Paid Protesters   63
    Stacie Swain

11. On the Tyranny of Individualism: MAGA Boy, Media,
    and the Drum   71
    Matt Sheedy

12. Symbols and Ownership   79
    Yasmine Flodin-Ali

13. Donald Trump: A "Baby Christian"?   83
    Leslie Dorrough Smith

14. An Orbiter Is a Simp, a Foid Is a Foid   87
    Nevada S. Drollinger-Smith

15. Naming Things   92
    Steven Ramey

16. While Whitey's on the Moon   96
    Annie Rose O'Brien

17. In Their Own Terms   102
    Vaia Touna

18. Shaking a Buddhist House of Cards   107
    Julia Oppermann

19. "A Good Fake or a Bad Fake?"   112
    Andie Alexander

20. Pay Attention!: Media, Performance, and Discourses
    on Authenticity   117
    Daniel Jones

21. Do People Misunderstand Their Own Religion?   125
    Craig Martin

Contents vii

22. But Is It Really Religion?   131
Savannah H. Finver

23. If It's Not Authentic, It's Not a Religion   135
Teemu Taira

24. Rebranding Religion: Authenticity, Representation, and the Marketplace   139
Zabeen Khamisa

25. Is There Neo-Nazi DNA?: Ancestry Tests and Biological Essentialism in American Racism   144
Martha Smith

26. Making Sense of a Sense of Self   149
Israel L. Domínguez

27. The Moves We Make   154
K. Merinda Simmons

28. Trans* Muslims and Jessica Krug: Analyzing the Discursive Power of Authenticity   159
Hinasahar Muneeruddin

Afterword: A Little Heritage Goes a Long Way   164
Andie Alexander and Jason W. M. Ellsworth

Index   178

Preface

> There is no such thing as identity, only operational acts of identification. The identities we talk about so pompously, as if they existed independently of those who express them, are made (and unmade) only through the mediation of such identificatory acts, in short, by their enunciation. (Bayart 2005: 92)

This volume's ability to exist rests within a larger project in which we are immersed, an international scholarly working group known as *Culture on the Edge* that began in the spring of 2012 as a collaborative of seven scholars at different career stages. We both started working with *Culture on the Edge* at later dates during different points of our graduate student lives. Andie, the Online Curator for *Culture on the Edge* since its inception, was blogging regularly for the *Studying Religion* in *Culture* blog based in the Department of Religious Studies at the University of Alabama. Jason began publishing articles with the blog during its second phase, known as Chapter 2. In 2017, we were both asked to become contributors during the third stage, known as Chapter 3. The central aim of the working group is to use social theory to offer more nuanced understandings of how those things that we commonly call "identities" are manufactured, managed, and continually reproduced—and doing so in a way that a wide readership can engage. The public face of the now 16-person collaborative is the *Culture on the Edge* Peer-Reviewed Blog, which was set up by and is maintained through the University of Alabama's College of Arts & Sciences' eTech Office.

The theoretical goal of *Culture on the Edge* aims to demonstrate the broader usefulness of our scholarly approach and critical examination of notions of identity. In looking at concepts and claims, *Culture on the Edge* examines the ways in which such claims of varied social groups are made, supported, and perpetuated with a particular focus on how they work to construct identities and social groups. More than

x   *Fabricating Authenticity*

an intellectual exercise, it is a focus on the construction of narratives allowing us to see the often unspoken politics that underscore some of our most common and naturalized claims. Demonstrating how a variety of critical tools that we each bring to the table from our perspective fields has relevance for a greater understanding of culture at large, *Culture on the Edge* examines the socio-political agendas, discrete strategies of identification, techniques, and stakes in an array of claims used to authorize or legitimize certain ways of living in the world. Building on the work of Jean-François Bayart, we contend that identity is necessarily a social phenomenon that is constantly being renegotiated rather than work from the presumption that identity is a mere description of an inner notion or sentiment, private and distinct from the public. Working from that foundation, the group examines a variety of social phenomena that work as productive examples, or e.g.s—to use the language of Jonathan Z. Smith—for larger questions about claims of identity (such as how the idea of authenticity is sometimes used to support them).

We have both benefitted from the professional mentorship of our *Edge* colleagues and want to continue in that vein. Our hope is that this collaboration works to engage varied scholarly perspectives and helps to demystify scholarship for broader audiences. Furthermore, the collaborative effort allows for scholars who might not otherwise overlap in terms of academic area of study to engage one another in questions and ideas that persist in the broader study of identification.

We would like to thank our colleagues at *Culture on the Edge* for being such engaged and supportive thinking partners, particularly Russell T. McCutcheon and Steven Ramey, who provided early advice on the trajectory of the volume. We want to thank Janet Joyce and Valerie Hall at Equinox Publishing Ltd. for their support of this volume and series, and we are grateful to their team for their work on this project. Finally, we are grateful to Vaia Touna, the series editor, for her interest and support in this volume as well as her helpful guidance in the process of developing it.

Jason W. M. Ellsworth, Dalhousie University & UPEI
Andie Alexander, Leibniz University Hannover

Introduction: Commodifying Authenticity

Jason W. M. Ellsworth and Andie Alexander

"Industrial societies are great factories of 'authenticity.'"
 – Jean-François Bayart (2005: 78)

"It's the Real Thing!"
 – *Coca-Cola*

The authentic can be defined in a number of manners, but often it posits something as an original instantiation or representative of that. Several synonyms guide a reference to the meaning of authenticity—real, pure, right, true, factual, genuine, natural, and bona fide. To further understand what might be considered "authentic," it can be helpful to think about what it supposedly *is not*—fake, faux, false, bogus, counterfeit, unreal, a sham, unnatural, or simply inauthentic. Deriving from the Greek *authentikós* (αὐθεντικός)—and yes, an etymology, or history of a word's derivation, is an origins narrative of authenticity in itself—authenticity refers to original or genuine, or to acting on one's own authority (*authéntēs,* or αὐθέντης). Thus, there is an authoritative nature to the classification of things or people as real or authentic, and claims of authenticity, much like authority, are often part of contested discourses steeped in power. Therefore, authority becomes a central focus for many in analyzing what and whose claims prevail. Anthropologist Eric Wolf reminds us that the act of meaning-making is one site to examine how competing power dynamics are constructed: "meanings are not imprinted into things by nature; they are developed and imposed by human beings. Several things follow from this. The ability to bestow meanings—to 'name' things, acts and ideas—is a source of power" (1982: 388). As Wolf

2   *Fabricating Authenticity*

continues though, naming something is not solely an act of legitimization; for the managers of ideology also obtain the ability from this discourse to deny the existence of the alternative categories—to render people "socially and symbolically invisible" (ibid.). As will be seen in this volume, in addition to people, one could also include organizations, brands, and objects in this line of argument. For example, claims about the authenticity of American-made cars, genuine Italian leather, or pure spring bottled water do not just promote the purported quality of those products but also demote or erase that of the competitors. In these market-based examples, this can lead to— if the claims are persuasive and work, that is—fewer competitors, hierarchies of acceptable purchases, and class divisions. Authenticity claims, then, have practical effects, are always political, and a site worthy of analysis.

This volume, in part, endeavors to demonstrate that claims of authenticity often are rooted in current socio-political issues. As such, we explore the social implications of authenticity claims so as to demonstrate the consequences they may have. Whether one is a fan of a prominent sports team or an adherent to a specific diet, they are very likely to encounter authenticity claims: "She's not a *real* soccer fan," or "he's not *really* a vegetarian." Such claims, seen here as a boundary policing device (i.e., delineating who is in and who is out of the group), are common social phenomena. Building on our work with *Culture on the Edge*, we approach this volume not with an understanding that there is some authentic nature to which identities should align; nor do the contributors have an interest in policing such boundaries. Rather, with our focus on identity construction, we examine how and why claims of authenticity are made. What issues provoked such a claim, and what is at stake in establishing those and not some other set of boundaries (for example, who gets to be a sports fan or a vegetarian)? The paired essays in this volume (one offering an analysis at a discrete site and the other a reply that presses the original piece just a bit further) work as conversation starters, using often mundane but quite useful examples to connect with and compare to other claims of authenticity. In fact, comparison is a necessary component of our studies, and our goal is to provide everyday examples of authenticity claims that can help to unpack notions of identity that are often taken for granted.

We follow the work of French sociologist and political scientist Jean-François Bayart, who, in his book *The Illusion of Cultural Identity*, states:

> Need it be said that determining the criteria for what is or is not "authentic" is always problematic? Authenticity is not established by the immanent properties of the phenomenon or object under consideration. It results from the perspective, full of desires and judgements, that is brought to bear on the past, in the eminently contemporary context in which one is situated. (2005: 78)

That the authenticity narrative is fabricated does not diminish the issues social actors raise with those narratives but instead to demonstrate the constructed aspect of what is or is not considered authentic—pointing to the *processes* and the hard work that is done by those very actors (whether intentionally or not) both in marking something as authentic and the stakes thereof. After all, like elsewhere, people in Italy eat all kinds of different things, making our idea here in North America of "authentic Italian food" a bit of a puzzling thing, if you think about it. Rather than view "authenticity" as pointing to something natural, we instead understand it to be a socially contested and constructed label that is used to manage and codify a variety of choices in relation to understandings of identity formation. One aspect of our contemporary context, at least here in North America, where fabrications of the authentic are hard to ignore, is in advertising and marketing campaigns. As noted by Bayart in the epigraph to this Introduction, "industrial societies are great factories of 'authenticity'" (ibid.: 78) that give us a starting point from which we can explore how we, as humans and social actors, construct our social worlds.

The Authenticity Market

A leisurely stroll through a bookstore on a Saturday morning with a coffee in hand seems like a rather mundane activity. Perusing a

4   *Fabricating Authenticity*

favorite section to find the latest from Margaret Atwood, a classic Hemmingway, or perhaps a children's book for the little one, bookstores today have something for everyone and are laid out in a well-researched and designed format to keep you shopping, buying—and sipping their eight-dollar lattes. From bestsellers to magazines, writing journals to motivational posters, and children's toys to adult games—the mega-chains particularly aim to have it all. One aspect of these stores that catches our attention is the seemingly endless array of self-help books marketed to transform oneself into a successful, strong member of society, often by finding one's so-called *true self.*

So not only can one buy the most recent edition of *National Geographic* or a James Patterson novel, one can also find their own "true" inner self by reading books such as *Something More: Excavating Your Authentic Self* (Breathnach 2000) or *Authentic: How to Be Yourself and Why It Matters* (Joseph 2016). The collection of titles is too long to list in this short introduction, but self-help book sections are populated with a spectrum of texts that claim connecting with one's authentic being will unleash aspects of ourselves such as that of an authentic leader or businessperson (Thacker 2016; Crofts 2003). Or they show how the use of crystals and Zen, with claims to ancient wisdom and modern science, can be used to connect with the authentic self (Bayda 2014; Singer 2019). These appeals to one's authentic nature and lifestyle employ a strategy for overcoming the obstacles one must face in life. Such appeals rest on the notion of an essential, stable self that, once tapped into, created, or rediscovered and revived, will provide access to or insight for solving all of one's problems in life. This, in part, is done by looking inward and then outwardly expressing one's presumed "inner self" that has somehow been deceived or repressed as a result of external stressors. Thus, these titles emphasize not only the importance of being one's authentic self, but also the need to correct one's fake or disingenuous behavior— i.e., many of these texts assert that individuals are betraying their authentic selves and should align their projected identity with their "true" essence. Rather than try to point out what is "real" or point to a specific internal or individual essence that is secondarily, outwardly expressed, we hope to draw attention here to how authenticity claims are rhetorical moves used to strategically essentialize and authorize competing (and sometimes contradictory) identities that one presents in society and how such authenticity claims are employed to legitimize certain ways of living over others.

While self-help books encourage readers to connect with an idea of a true or authentic self, we do not wish to single them out. Turn down another aisle of that same bookstore and walk through the food section, and you'll find endless titles referencing authentic national recipes such as this Chinese cookbook, *Essential Chinese Cooking: Authentic Chinese Recipes, Broken Down Into Easy Techniques* (Pang 2016). Recipe books, not to mention restaurants themselves, purport authenticity at every corner, but often that "authenticity" is rooted more in the local context of the restaurant. For instance, Outback Steakhouse, an American chain known for its Australian-themed cuisine, features a signature dish called the Bloomin' Onion, which was first created in the United States by Outback founder Tim Gannon in 1988 (Outback Steakhouse n.d.). While unfamiliar to many Australians, this dish, developed and popularized by the American owner, plays a vital role creating the restaurant's authentic Aussie ambiance. Accordingly, these appeals to national authenticity connect both to business interests (after all, they are selling a product) and to notions of national identity and heritage.

Whether marketing authentic Jamaican recipes or real Mexican tacos, such national or cultural recipe books and restaurants present themselves as representative of a particular heritage or culture. However, those "authentic" representations are not as self-evident as they might appear. For instance, consider the on-going debates in the U.S. South regarding the best or most authentic barbeque (referring here to the food and not the cooking equipment). Conceptions of authentic BBQ vary significantly by location—after all, Texas BBQ is nothing like that of Kansas City or Tennessee. Determining which style of BBQ is superior or the most authentic depends largely on where one is from, as many individuals—though certainly not all—tend to favor the style with which they are most familiar. In this sense, authenticity is often tied more to familiarity rather than the so-called objective quality of the food.

Assertions of authentic representations of national heritage do similar authorizing work. As the late scholar of religion Jonathan

6   *Fabricating Authenticity*

Z. Smith argues, the representative selection of foods is a "radical, almost arbitrary, selection out of the incredible number of potential sources of nutriment" (1982: 40–41). The subsequent reduction of those limited foods to that of a cultural cuisine is a "phenomenon characterized by variegation" wherein the reduction, or limitation, is overcome by an "exercise of ingenuity" which "introduce[s] interest and variety ... usually accompanied by a complex set of rules" (ibid.). As such, we can understand that a U.S.-based Mexican taqueria's claims to cooking the most authentic Mexican food works to establish the restaurant as providing a cultural connection and maintaining a specific type of Mexican heritage (because that, too, varies regionally) distinct from that of the American culture in which it is embedded. These claims, then, are not necessarily about the food itself (or the recipes in cookbooks) but rather the identity and distinction they help to cultivate or maintain. By shifting our focus to see what is at stake in making these claims, we find that assertions of authenticity tell us far more about those making the claims than they do about some essential quality of a product (Spooner 1988). As further argued by scholars of religion Aaron W. Hughes and Russell T. McCutcheon in their entry on "Authenticity" in *Religion in 50 Words: A Critical Vocabulary*, "Claims that either this or that is the authentic form of some religion should prompt us to scrutinize the interests of the one who makes such a claim about the world and to investigate the effects of employing it, should its use be heard as persuasive and uncontested" (2021: 22). These sites of marketing, food, national identity, or religion, then, are not that different from one another when examining claims to the authentic—something that will become more apparent as this volume unfolds.

We understand authenticity discourses as a comparative practice used for differentiating two or more things from one another (in this case, a busy economy) so to legitimize or authorize one over the other—for example, authentic vs. inauthentic, real vs. fake, internal vs. external. The analysis in this volume takes the claims of authenticity—as well as the myriad of terms falling under this umbrella—as a productive site for critical inquiry. These othering discourses separate the self and other (us vs. them). Reframing our questions from those of authenticity and instead to *claims* of authenticity allows us to focus on how boundaries are drawn, which identities are authorized and delegitimized, and who benefits from the subsequent delineation.

Given the prevalence of authenticity claims in current marketing practices, what might we make of the history of such rhetorical strategies in advertising? The origins of employing authenticity claims in advertising is itself an attempt to construct an origins narrative which authorizes present-day agendas. So rather than reproducing what it is we're wanting to unpack, let's instead explore one prominent example from the 1970s when U.S. advertising giant McCann Erickson (now known as McCann Worldgroup) came up with a way to bottle the notion of authenticity in what is still viewed as one of the most iconic advertising campaigns of all time: *It's the Real Thing!* The once well-known TV commercial, featuring the song "Buy the World a Coke," ends with a statement appearing on the screen: "On a hilltop in Italy, we assembled young people from all over the world... to bring you this message from Coca-Cola Bottlers all over the world 'It's the real thing. Coke'" (Backer et al. 1971). So successful, and even iconic, that the television series *Mad Men* used the commercial as the series-ending final ad campaign to enshrine fictional character Don Draper as the greatest advertising person of his time (Weiner 2015).

As explained on the *Coca-Cola* website, the story to this ad was born in 1971 during heavy fog in London when a flight carrying Bill Backer of McCann Erickson was diverted to Shannon, Ireland. With few hotels in sight, it was not ideal:

> Many passengers were upset and frustrated, which led to a few raised voices. Bill saw some of the most vocal passengers from the night before laughing and sharing stories with their new friends over bottles of Cokes. He saw the bottle of Coke as a small moment of pleasure that allowed people to share happiness. Motivated by the scene, he picked up a napkin and wrote the line: "I'd like to buy the world a Coke and keep it company." (Ryan n.d.)

Backer, working with Roger Cook, Billy Davis, and Roger Greenaway, produced Coke's jingle "Buy the World a Coke" sung by The New Seekers and released in February 1971. The song would become the centerpiece to Coca-Cola's "Hilltop" commercial featuring an ethnically, racially, and culturally diverse group of people presenting a

8   *Fabricating Authenticity*

world in unison. In the ad, the group comes together around bottles of Coke, supposedly leaving their differences aside, finding moments of harmony, and representing *authentic connections*—that is, deeply felt, sincere, real, etc. (Backer et al. 1971).

The commercial itself is a helpful example for unpacking notions of authenticity. On that hilltop, the singers are dressed in what one might describe as "traditional" or "authentic" attire specific to the region, country, or culture they are meant to represent. Marked by their clothing, each person is presented as a distinct individual (rather than a homogenous group), who has joined this diverse gathering on a hilltop to share a Coke, highlighting the ways in which Coca-Cola brings people together (ibid.). While one can appreciate the sentiment, it is worth addressing how the ad emphasizes those cultural and national differences to make evident Coke's universal ability to bring people together (and consequently, not Pepsi's). That universality is highlighted further by having the Coca-Cola label appear in different languages on the various Coke bottles. For a 21st century audience, it is difficult to ignore the stereotypes presented in the video. Considering that 1970s fashion in Japan, for example, did not differ that greatly from that of the U.S., having a young woman wear a kimono suggests that the differences highlighted in the video are steeped in their own issues of what "authentic Japanese culture" looks like. But in shifting our attention somewhat, we can instead examine *how* those differences are constructed for this particular ad to understand how Coke effectively positions itself as that one "real thing" that helps bridge those differences to create a sense of shared community and identity for the formerly disconnected individuals.

But what is this "real thing" being discussed? For the company selling soda, the answer is easy: Coca-Cola. However, if we look at the song from which both the lyrics and melody in part derived, "True Love and Apple Pie," sung by Susan Shirley and also written by Cook and Greenaway, we find something different. The version sung by Shirley (1971), depicts someone yearning for a "sweet old home" of their own:

> Don't promise me no diamond rings, or castles in the sky; just real life things like … true love and apple pie.

So here, in Shirley's version, all the "real life things" are simple pleasures like love and apple pie. Shirley's song could be classified as almost anti-consumerist, whereas Coca-Cola's "Hilltop" commercial shifts the interests to that of purchasing and marketing. The commercial highlights individual differences and markets Coca-Cola as a solution to overcoming them and for bringing people together. As sung in the opening line of the song "Buy the World a Coke" (Backer et al. 1971):

I'd like to *buy* the world a home...

Another later rewrite of the Coca-Cola jingle into the pop song "I'd Like to Teach the World to Sing (In Perfect Harmony)" (Hillside Singers 1971) emphasizes an imagined community *building,* not buying, a better world with a subtle change in the opening line:

I'd like to *build* the world a home...

An easy critique of this reading might be that Coke's song is disingenuous and that Shirley's version or other later versions are somehow more authentic or genuine. But our goal is to dissuade you of such knee-jerk reactions and to instead reflect on how effectively Coca-Cola employed a song about world harmony for marketing purposes. The success for Coke was branding that "genuine" moment in an advertising campaign by showing how one could *buy* that "real thing" in a bottle at a vending machine nearby. But it is not just Coca-Cola that is being promoted. Here, the very act of buying and consuming are presented as avenues for social change. Thus, this is also about justifying the pervading economic systems that the Coca-Cola company relies on to produce profits—that is, capitalism.

On a planet where commodities travel across the globe in long supply chains before being purchased, the *origins* of a product becomes particularly important for getting consumers to relate to it further. To do so, authenticity claims are often deployed to move beyond the seemingly impersonal (read: corporate) to the personal— a product with which one can identify with and that goes beyond mere words. For example, take the bottle of vino named *Farmers*

10   *Fabricating Authenticity*

of Wine that labels its bottle with authenticity not once, not twice, but three times—"authentic tradition," "crafted with authentic Italian grapes," and made by the most "authentic farmers." However, it is not only the words on the label that work to establish its authenticity. In this instance, a brown, paper-bag label engulfs the bottle and features an image of what appears to be farmer's hands gently cradling soil. This connection not only evokes the presence of a real farmer but also distinguishes the product from merely being associated with an industrial production line. A vine emerging from the soil, symbolically pointing to the wine's origins—the growth of the very plant responsible for producing the grapes in the wine. In other words, we see here that it is not just words that are operationalized but a bundle of techniques (such as the label and images)—what Bayart names "operational acts"—that work together towards this effect. Thus, it is also how material objects are constructed and operationalized with these very claims in mind. As will be evident in the following chapters, these operational acts and bundles of techniques together demonstrate how we, as humans, are continually fabricating the authentic for specific ends. The use of narratives, images, and material objects to construct a bundled claim of authenticity, naturalness, and origins works to (re)establish an identity for a product and the consumer who drinks it. In other words, claims to authenticity are used to authorize identities—and in this instance, to help sell a bottle of wine.

Beyond food, marketing authenticity is key to the fashion, clothing, and art industries. Despite the high cost, corporations work to ensure you only buy trademarked and licensed apparel. For instance, the socio-economic status associated with purchasing or owning authentic Gucci versus the faux one sold on the street corner in New York City allows one to demonstrate their status by owning *genuine*, name-brand products instead of the cheaper *knockoffs*. Similarly, authentic prints (which are themselves copies, no?) of famous works of art offer yet another site for examining how authenticity is constructed. The question of legitimacy is raised depending on the mode of production: which copies are legitimate reprintings and which are forgeries? They are both copies, but the latter is regarded as inauthentic or fake. For example, much of Andy Warhol's art was mass-produced from "The Factory" using a silkscreen technique. This method made it possible for Warhol's assistants to produce the art—rather than Warhol himself—which stirred controversy about which pieces of artwork were "authentic Warhols." But unlike forgeries, these mass-produced prints from various artists are still regarded as Warhols in museums and consumer marketplaces alike.

Rather than delving further into a critique of marketing, we instead suggest that such advertisements are quite effective, and discourses of "authenticity" are thriving within the marketplace. The advertising industry knows the power of these claims, and the thirst for these *genuine* products is capitalized on in a number of industries. Firmenich, one of the world's largest fragrance and flavor production companies, notes that consumers demand "authentic" tasting food and "natural" products (2021). Perhaps for a company that manufactures flavors, the emphasis is to claim that the products are not somehow fake so as to get consumers to buy into the idea that what they consume is a "true" experience, no matter the manufacturing line on which it was produced. If the saying that "you are what you eat" is correct, then perhaps the narratives and claims about the food we eat *are* tied to one's identity—that is, you are the discourses you consume. By eating, or more broadly consuming, things that are claimed to be more authentic or real, these become claims about one's own "realness."

Fabricating Authenticity

This volume is not in search of "The Real Thing." Instead, it is interested in how claims of authenticity operate in the present. And while the world of advertising is a pervading presence in our lives today under global capitalism, this volume is not solely about brands, commodities, or corporations but instead is about people—specifically, how people are identified, classified, and divided. Thinking back to our understanding of authenticity rhetoric working to establish boundaries between "us" and "them," consider this argument from anthropologist Regina Bendix's *In Search of Authenticity: The Formation of Folklore Studies*: "Authenticity, unlike 'primitive society,' is generated not from the bounded classification of an Other but from the probing comparison between self and other, as well as between

12   *Fabricating Authenticity*

external and internal states of being" (1997: 17). Here it is not about a stable object of study that can be observed "in its own terms" (Touna, Chapter 17) as something authentic from the past, but instead is focused on the space *between* authentic and inauthentic (or self and other). The "and," the "or," or the "vs." It is within the notion of what it means to be "modern" that the foil of the Other is created for consumption. However, it is important to note that authenticity claims can also point toward a counter-process aimed at reclaiming what has been seemingly appropriated or stolen. And yet, as demonstrated in this volume, these assertions are rooted in current socio-political issues, necessitating the examination of the broader consequences and impacts, akin to any other claim. This type of analysis is not to delegitimize the social impact and consequences of these moments but rather to take seriously how much work is going on at these sites. For in recognizing "culture" as a socially constructed phenomenon, we are also interested in when and how claims of appropriation are made (and consequently, when they are not). Critically examining the agonistic moments of these claims can also allow one to engage with the broader societal issues driving this or that particular moment of contest.

While some academic work addresses the discourse of authenticity directly (for example, see Bendix 1997; Fillitz and Saris 2012), scholars across the humanities have been complicit at times in reifying the very category. While this is certainly true of much work from the past, anthropologists Thomas Fillitz and A. Jamie Saris note that the "spectre of authenticity" is a ghostly presence found in the field of anthropology (2012: 8). Though it should be noted that many academic fields and disciplines are entwined in the very legitimization process of a variety of authenticity narratives and political discourses—trying to strike a balance between representation and legitimacy. In this way, scholarship has a history of being complicit in validating the very claims to authenticity that are made in the world. Instead, this volume endeavors to move in another direction, that is, to complicate and problematize discourses of authenticity, which are otherwise left unexamined or even taken at face value, so as to understand what is at stake in those very discourses.

ELLSWORTH AND ALEXANDER *Introduction* 13

To grapple with and complicate claims of authenticity as discursive moments of social contest, we have collected our main chapters from members of *Culture on the Edge*. In these short pieces, the contributors draw on a variety of topics and ideas that one might encounter ranging from politics to pop culture—and everything in between—to unpack and critically engage the discourses of authenticity at work in their topics and to explore the circumstances in which they emerged. Following the format of the other volumes in this series, we have invited early-career scholars to respond to the main chapters of this volume. Their reflections and analyses take the argument in a new direction by applying it to yet another instance of authenticity claims and entertaining, in a variety of examples, the complexity of naming something as "authentic," which proves to be neither a simple nor self-evident process. It is this *process* (i.e., the on-going contest of authenticity claims and the issues that provoked it) that the chapters of this volume examine as sites of meaning-*making* and identity construction. Our hope is that these brief examples work as productive starting points and models for rethinking how claims of authenticity pervade our social worlds.

Jason W. M. Ellsworth is a doctoral candidate in the Sociology and Social Anthropology Department at Dalhousie University. He currently works at the Faculty of Medicine at the University of Prince Edward Island and serves on the Executive Committee of the Canadian Anthropology Society. His research explores a diverse array of topics including the Anthropology and Sociology of Religion, Buddhism in North America, Food and Food Movements, Theories of Value, Political Economy, Marketing, Transnationalism, and Orientalism.

Andie Alexander is a doctoral candidate in the Institute for the Study of Religion at Leibniz University Hannover and is Managing Editor of *The Religious Studies Project*. Her research focuses on identity construction, discourses of difference and experience, and conceptions of the individual as a way of examining how post-9/11 discourses of inclusivity and pluralism implicitly work as a form of governance and subject-making which construct and constrain the liberal Muslim subject.

14   *Fabricating Authenticity*

References

Backer, Bill, et al. (1971). *Hilltop*. Metromedia, July 1971. YouTube video, 01:14. Posted 6 March 2012. Retrieved from https://www.youtube.com/watch?v=1VM2eLhvsSM (accessed 20 November 2019).

Bayart, Jean-François (2005) [1996]. *The Illusion of Cultural Identity*. Chicago: University of Chicago Press.

Bayda, Ezra (2014). *The Authentic Life: Zen Wisdom For Living Free from Complacency and Fear*. Boston, MA: Shambhala.

Bendix, Regina (1997). *In Search of Authenticity: The Formation of Folklore Studies*. Madison, WI: The University of Wisconsin Press.

Breathnach, Sarah Ban (2000). *Something More: Excavating Your Authentic Self*. Grand Central Publishing.

Crofts, Neil (2003). *Authentic: How to Make a Living by Being Yourself*. Chichester, West Sussex: Capstone.

Fillitz, Thomas, and A. Jamie Saris (2012). *Debating Authenticity: Concepts of Modernity in Anthropological Perspective*. New York, NY: Berghahn.

Firmenich (2021). "Firmenich Unveils Innovative Collection of All-Natural Citrus Oils Delivering Unique Freshness & Authenticity." *Firmenich*. Retrieved from https://www.firmenich.com/taste-and-beyond/press-release/firmenich-unveils-innovative-collection-all-natural-citrus-oils (accessed 20 November 2019).

Hillside Singers, The (1971). *I'd Like to Teach the World to Sing*. Metromedia Records. November 1971. Vinyl.

Hughes, Aaron W., and Russell T. McCutcheon (2021). *Religion in 50 Words: A Critical Vocabulary*. London and New York: Routledge.

Joseph, Stephen (2016). *Authentic: How to Be Yourself and Why It Matters*. London: Piatkus Books.

Outback Steakhouse (n.d.). "The Original: Bloomin' Onion." *Outback Steakhouse*. Retrieved from https://www.outback.com/offers/bloomin-onion (accessed 20 November 2019).

Pang, Jeremy (2016). *Essential Chinese Cooking: Authentic Chinese Recipes, Broken Down into Easy Techniques*. Quadrille Pub.

Ryan, Ted (n.d.). "I'd Like to Buy the World a Coke: The Story Behind the Famous Song." *Coca-Cola*. Retrieved from (web archive) https://web.archive.org/web/20180320143653/http://www.coca-cola.ie/Blog/i-d-like-to-buy-the-world-a-coke (accessed 7 December 2023).

Shirley, Susan (1971). "True Love and Apple Pie." Columbia. May 1971. Vinyl.

Singer, Beatriz (2019). *Crystal Blueprint: Reconnect with Your Authentic Self Through the Ancient Wisdom and Modern Science of Quartz Crystals.* Carlsbad, CA: Hay House, Inc.

Smith, Jonathan Z. (1982). *Imagining Religion: From Babylon to Jonestown.* Chicago: University of Chicago Press.

Spooner, Brian (1988). "Weavers and Dealers: The Authenticity of an Oriental Carpet." In Arjun Appadurai (ed.), *The Social Life of Things: Commodities in Cultural Perspective*, 195–235. Cambridge: Cambridge University Press.

Thacker, Karrisa (2016). *The Art of Authenticity: Tools to Become an Authentic Leader and Your Best Self.* Hoboken, NJ: Wiley.

Weiner, Matthew, dir. (2015). *Mad Men.* "Person to Person," season 7, episode 14. Weiner Bros. Productions. Aired 17 May 2015 on AMC.

Wolf, Eric (1982). *Europe and the People Without History.* Berkeley and Los Angeles, CA: University of California Press.

1. Is There Lettuce in a Greek Salad?

Russell T. McCutcheon

I love Greek food. The crisp, thin slices of lightly battered deep fried zucchini, the tender grilled octopus with olive oil and lemon squeezed on it just as it's served, the stuffed grape leaves—I could go on (and on...)—all served on little plates, brought to the table one after another, and all accompanied by good, fresh bread. Yes, I love Greek food.

I first went to Greece in 2006, for nearly a week, to attend an academic conference in the northern city of Thessaloniki, their second largest city (behind the capital, Athens, of course), and although I'd certainly had my share of things that, for example, I had called "a Greek salad" prior to sitting down at an outdoor café, near the sea, I'd never really eaten anything that I guess I'd say was *authentically* Greek. I had such a good experience that I went back, two years later, and this time I brought along some students, then again the next year with more undergrads from our Department, and before you knew it I'd gone back six or seven times, developed some great friendships, visited a number of museum and archeological sites in the north, spent some time in a village or two, and even drove a little rental car part ways up Mt. Olympus's narrow gravel roads. And with each trip I ate more grape leaves, learned to call them *dolmas*, and even started making them at home for myself, back in Alabama. And of course I'd brag to all of my friends back in Greece about my cross-cultural cooking exploits—one of whom was Vaia Touna, who I first met in Greece when she was a graduate student, and with whom I now work in Alabama; for I'd found a recipe in one of Mark Bittman's cookbooks (he's the well-known food columnist for *The New York Times*), and so I partially cooked the rice and onion, then added the spices along with handfuls of chopped parsley and mint, blended the toasted pine nuts and currants, as well as the ground lamb that I'd already cooked. I then placed a small spoonful of the cooked stuffing into the grape leaves that came in a jar (yes, I even trimmed off the small, woody stem) and then rolled each and boiled a big batch, all arranged so nicely in our large pot, in order to enjoy those delicious treats all week.

An authentic taste of Greece in Alabama.

During one of those playful boasting sessions I proudly reported back to Thessaloniki how I had made my grape leaves (yes, I'm sure that I also posted a picture or two online), much like I did in the above paragraph—probably wanting some confirmation that I was on the right track and more than likely also hoping that my kitchen labors were seen as a thank you to them for how wonderfully I had been hosted while there. By then I'd become good friends with Vaia and her family; because only she spoke both English and Greek, she would relay my cooking small-talk to her mother—who was, in my books at least, the expert on all things culinary. Although I don't speak Greek—sure, I can say hello, thank you, and good morning, even "My name is Russell. What's your name?"—it was clear that something was wrong as soon as she related my recipe's ingredients to her mom. I can only imagine the cognitive dissonance—which, I imagine, sounds like the proverbial record needle scratching across the album—that was occasioned by everyone learning that I had included pine nuts...? And currants...? Even lamb...?

These were *not* authentic *dolmas*.

But it gets more complicated, for I had by then also learned that even calling them "*dolmas*" was an issue, since the long history of, shall we say, complex interactions between what was once called the Ottoman Empire (which reigned in the region from 1299 to 1923, a fragment of which is the modern nation-state of Turkey) and Greece meant that all sorts of things were shared among people in this region who otherwise saw themselves as different—from food and elements of language to a variety of cultural practices. Though we find stuffed and rolled grape leaves all across this region—from the Middle East to parts of Asia, in fact—*dolmas* is, as I came to understand it, a term

18   *Fabricating Authenticity*

of Turkish origin (meaning something that is stuffed), which is distinguished from the term "*sarma*," which more specifically names a stuffed and rolled vegetable leaf (like cabbage rolls, another variant in the region on this same sort of dish—something I associate with Hungarian immigrants who settled near to where I was born and raised in southern Ontario, near Toronto); but in Greece, even though the Turkish name is obviously well-known (since the Ottomans had occupied the territory that we think of today as modern Greece for about four hundred years—an occupation that slowly ended, region by region, across much of the 19th and early 20th century, e.g., while Greece was recognized as a sovereign state in 1832, with the Treaty of Constantinople, its north, including Thessaloniki, was not captured by Greeks until late 1912), there's a good chance they're instead termed *dolmades*, *dolmadakia*, or even *sarmadakia*.

So if I was going for authentic Greek *dolmas* the problem wasn't just the lamb and currants that I was adding—though that was indeed a problem, one we joke about to this day, when Vaia's mother, Martha, happily scolds me by wagging her finger at me on Skype, whenever I tease her about the meat in my recipe—but the very name that I was calling them was, unbeknownst to me, undermining the presumed authenticity of the dish. For in that very moment when one chooses to say either *dolmades* or *dolmas*, or whether to add meat or just stick with rice and herbs, a host of complex topics are lurking just below the surface, from understandably and still present hard feelings for what one's ancestors went through while under what they considered to be foreign, Ottoman domination to ongoing contests over who originated what and thus who copied whom.

But for my taste buds, the lamb is crucial, the pine nuts give it a little crunch, and the sweetness of the currants brings it all together— a sweetness that, I'm told by those from elsewhere, is quite characteristic of much of the North American cuisine. (Corn syrup seems to be on every second ingredients label, after all.) In fact, my wife agrees, so that if we make them any other way we feel a little let down, like we've somehow deviated from the norm, as if we've made an inauthentic dish. Yet back in Thessaloniki, my grape leaves would likely not be seen as proper at all and would, probably, instead be seen as bearing all the marks of a North American palate. But, come to think

McCutcheon *Is There Lettuce in a Greek Salad?* 19

of it, presumably there's as many ways to make these little appetizers, even within Greece itself, as there are Greek cooks—each putting their own variation on the small number of staple ingredients that go into the dish, perhaps representing their own innovation or, maybe, preserving something taught to them that may distinguish their own family's recipe from those of others. And each results in something that, should it be altered, produces a taste that's somehow not quite right.

A taste that's improper, impure, derivative—in a word, inauthentic.

Case in point: consider a story that Vaia herself once related to me when she confessed that:

> I have no idea in which situations we use which of these terms: *o dolmas* (singular; a rare usage); *oi dolmades* (plural); *to dolmadaki* (singular; the -aki suffix means something small); *ta dolmadakia* (plural); *o sarmas* (singular; I've never heard people using it); *to sarmadaki* (singular; again, the diminutive suffix); *ta sarmadakia* (plural), etc. It all depends on regions in Greece, I think, for you will often hear these terms all used interchangeably. A friend in Canada, at the University of Alberta, who was from Athens, once corrected me when I used the term *sarmadakia* to name what he was making because he was adding meat and he told me that they were called *dolmades* or *dolmadakia*, and then when I told him that in Thessaloniki we don't add meat he said, "Oh, you are making *dolmadakia yalantzi*" (a term from Turkish, meaning fake *dolmadakia*).

Even Greeks—as, I conjecture, would members of any nationality, given how many regional differences are subsumed within the idealized national whole—seem to disagree about what is authentically Greek. But if we pay careful attention to the situation of this friendly dispute—two Greek citizens, each from different parts of that country, who are both displaced significantly by attending university in the wintery north of western Canada, each periodically cooking nostalgic reminders of familiar tastes, conjuring memories (as we all do) of where they're from and with whom they most intimately identify...—well, you then start to get a sense that the conversation about what to call, and how to make, those little rolled grape leaves

20 *Fabricating Authenticity*

may in fact have little to do with the dish itself and, instead, have everything to do with social actors who are doing the cooking, cooks working in an obviously competitive social market, social actors re-creating a sense of who they are, to whom they're related, and thus who they're not.

And doing it all by means of—among many other things, for sure—what goes into this or that dish and what they call it.

This notion of local variation in the midst of identifying something as unique or one of a kind, was nicely exemplified for me by yet another occasion in Greece, when I learned that our common tendency here, of putting lettuce into a Greek salad, was *not* practiced there at all. That a Greek salad is hardly called a Greek salad in Greece (much as, or so the old joke goes, Chinese food is just called food in China) should be obvious, but maybe it isn't. It's more than likely called a "rustic salad" (Greek: *horiatiki*) or maybe even a "tomato salad" and generally has roughly diced tomatoes (which go into the bowl first, as I was precisely instructed!), followed by cucumbers, olives, a little red onion along with, of course, feta. Like feta itself—which has jokingly been described to me not as one type of cheese but as, what else, feta!—a rustic salad struck me as being close to a national dish, something of great pride and simple significance. Sprinkle a little oregano and olive oil on top, then also some vinegar perhaps, and voila, an authentic Greek classic is born. But here in North America, where I guess we reinvent it to suit ourselves, I've seen all sorts of other things added to what a restaurant's menu calls an "Authentic Greek Salad"—lettuce and hot peppers being high on the list of add-ons. So, given what I had become accustomed to in either Canada or the U.S., on my first trip to Greece I was surprised to find no lettuce; after all, lettuce = salad for many of us here, no? (Even chicken salad or egg salad are often both served on a bed of iceberg lettuce, after all.) Yet again, the improper North Americanization of a foreign dish became all too apparent to me (at least we didn't add any corn syrup, I guess)—until…, that is, I dined at Vaia's home and, among other wonderful dishes that her mother had made there was also, yes, a rustic salad in a big bowl on the table.

It had lettuce in it.

McCutcheon *Is There Lettuce in a Greek Salad?* 21

Fresh from the lecture about no meat in the grape leaves, I was probably emboldened and so I recall poking a little fun about the inappropriate use of lettuce. Martha's quick-witted reply?

It's my house; I can add what I like.

What a rich moment that was—innovation and conservation (all woven together into a moment in which one claims ownership, identity, and thus place), two crucial elements of any cultural performance; for they are the mechanisms by which we create the sense of both continuity and uniformity while reserving for ourselves a domain of unique singularity: we are the same but I am me, nonetheless. We share much but I make my stand here. Thinking of that moment, and sticking with my Greek culinary examples, may help us to understand how innumerable people all can quite sincerely claim to be making authentic Greek food, yet all may be preparing a variety of different things that vary—probably within specific and maybe even predictable ways—in either this or that manner. Studying claims of authenticity—moments when issues of purity, origination, and direct lineage are advanced and, inevitably, debated—and examining situations (much as those already mentioned) in which issues of ownership, authority, and identity are asserted and contested, are thus among the most interesting opportunities that scholars can have, I think, so long as they are interested in how it is that people the world over continually work, often in competition with each other, to turn their generic environments into meaningful and manageable settings where we can make our homes, raise families, have lives, and, in the process, mark and police territory as ours and ours alone.

After all, just how does one make a delimited collection of ingredients taste properly *Greek*, yet then, with a little tweaking, taste Italian or Moroccan or maybe Middle Eastern...? For yes, there are many ways to make a salad, but *this and only this* shall constitute a Greek salad—but I, of course, reserve the right to add lettuce when it either suits my tastes or when I happen to have it on hand; for a rustic or peasant salad isn't something fancy and probably derives from simple, plain ingredients that just happen to be in the garden or, today, in the fridge. In fact, was Martha even aiming to make an identity claim by

22   *Fabricating Authenticity*

adding that salad to our meal or did that bowl simply contain what a gracious host happened to have at hand, was able to offer a guest, suggesting that while she put a salad on the table, I'm the one who put identity on the table with my comment about the lettuce. With that and the other above examples in mind, let us then think of claims of authenticity—the positions from which we pronounce others as faking it—as evidence of adjustments and negotiations, situations in which we try to gain a competitive edge for ourselves and those that we, at least for the moment and in this particular setting, consider to be like us or not—an effort to set our grape leaves (and thereby ourselves) apart by adding meat.

But be careful never to add too much, of course.

Which brings me to one last story about cooking that I'll tell: our cooking experiments have not ended with grape leaves, of course, for we have a wonderful Greek cookbook, a gift from Vaia and her family, that we regularly use. We found a nice recipe for a variation on stuffed grape leaves, using small pieces of white fish as a filling instead of rice and herbs; it's called *Psari se Klimatofila*, or fish in grape leaves. After making it, we once again proudly bragged to our friends back in Thessaloniki about what we'd prepared (though we failed to say where we'd found the recipe). When Vaia shared the news with her brother that we had just prepared fish wrapped in grape leaves they both found it an extremely strange dish to make and, as told to us, he simply commented (in Greek):

Now they've gone too far!

That the dish came from the Greek cookbook *that they had sent to us*, from Greece, and that it was therefore as Greek a dish as any, at least according to the well-known cook who had written the book—Vefa Alexiadou (Βεφα Αλεξιαδου, in Greek)—and that the book's cover proclaimed it to be "The bible of authentic Greek cooking," made this boundary judgment on limitation and variation too rich not to cite here. For despite the cookbook's introductory claim that its recipes all exhibit "remarkable continuity" with the ancient Greek past, the contemporary regional variations collected together in its pages, not unlike the dispute over whether Athenians and Thessalonikians put meat in their *dolmades*, make evident that authenticity, and so too identity, is rather more complicated than it might first appear.

Fake grape leaves…, going too far…, are both instances of people policing the edges and risking their own place should they exceed them. All this is wrapped up in claims to authenticity.

So instead of tasting a dish to determine if it conforms to the original, rather than looking closely at a painting to figure out if it is indeed authentic, and instead of trying to trace your family's lineage to prove your legitimacy, maybe we should instead turn our attention to the cooks tasting the dish, the art critic gazing at the portrait, and the genealogy experts deciding which of the many family lines to trace—those whose decisions and interests determine *what gets to count* as the essential character, the original form, and thus the boundary across which none shall apparently pass. For their claims of legitimacy and rank, and the objects those claims produce and authorize, may not, as we sometimes think, be innocent descriptions of obvious facts but, instead, may be evidence of arm-wrestling matches in the here-and-now that, if you're not careful, you'll end up overlooking.

For it turns out a that Greek salad does and doesn't have lettuce in it.

Russell T. McCutcheon is University Research Professor in the Department of Religious Studies at the University of Alabama. He has written widely, over the past 30 years, on issues of relevance to the methods and theories used in the academic study of religion, among which has been how social actors use the rhetoric of authenticity to legitimize their claims.

2. Beyond Authenticity?

Ian Alexander Cuthbertson

Authenticity claims often depend on three related ideas: authority, origin(s), and tradition(s). The things in the world that earn the designation "authentic" tend to be those that apparently match an imagined original prototype or else seem to fit with an imagined procedure as judged by someone who is (or at least appears to be) competent to make such determinations. For me, the most interesting question is never whether a particular thing (a salad, for instance) *really is* authentic or inauthentic but rather *how* and *why* and by *whom* it is designated as such. I'm also interested in *when* authenticity claims are possible or meaningful (or not) in the first place.

Trust Me

The "why" of authenticity claims often involves, as Russell McCutcheon notes, attempts to gain a "competitive edge." Sticking with food examples (because who doesn't love food?), foodies and food tourists alike are usually interested in acquiring "authentic" experiences and tasting "authentic" food. This itself can become a kind of competition as each foodie strives to display tasteful photos of ever more authentic (and exotic) dishes on social media as means of demonstrating their culinary capital, or their social worth as measured by particular kinds of expertise coupled with their ability to make nuanced distinctions as connoisseurs (Guptill et al. 2017: 36–38).

But restaurants and restauranteurs also seek a competitive edge via claims of authenticity. To provide just one example, in season 5 episode 3 of the Netflix series *Chef's Table*, Thai Chef Bo Songvisava (who learned how to cook Thai food under the tutelage of Australian

Chef David Thompson at Nahm in London) claims that whereas other restaurants in Thailand cater to European palates, her own restaurant Bo.Lan is unique in that it provides *authentic* Thai food (Fried 2018). Having eaten at Bo.Lan, I can attest to the fact that the food is excellent. But who am I (or for that matter who is Bo Songvisava) to claim that her food is not just delicious but *authentic* as well?

The "who am I?" question hinges on the notion of authority. Is Bo Songvisava more authoritative on the authenticity of her food (or less so?) given that she has a vested interest in presenting the food she cooks as authentic (and therefore worth the hefty price Bo.Lan charges)? Does the fact that McCutcheon has (allegedly) visited Greece "six or seven times" make him more authoritative on the topic of Greece and Greek salads? What about the fact the first recipe he describes comes from a "well-known" food columnist working at a *major* U.S. newspaper (*The New York Times*)? Would we trust the recipe less if an unknown food blogger had posted it on an obscure website? The point here isn't simply to doubt the facts presented (I'm pretty sure McCutcheon has, in fact, visited Greece), but to notice that these elements are examples of the kind of posturing or arm-wrestling McCutcheon describes.

Origin and Obscurity

The concept of origins plays out differently in different realms of human production. Sometimes, distinctions between "*the* original" and various reproductions, copies, or remixes seem to be relatively clear, and determinations concerning which object came first are consequential. Whether or not a particular painting was actually made by Picasso or whether it is merely in the style of the artist will affect that painting's perceived value (both artistically and monetarily).

The world of food complicates the idea of origins because many prepared foods predate written records. Consider Pizza. The invention of pizza is usually credited to the Italian baker Raffaele Esposito who created a pizza to honor King Umberto I and Queen Margherita in 1889. The pizza's toppings (tomato sauce, mozzarella, and basil) represented what would eventually become the flag of the Kingdom

26   *Fabricating Authenticity*

of Italy in 1861. Yet the constituent components of pizza (flatbread, cheese, tomatoes, basil) had existed in what would become Italy for centuries. Flatbread and cheese had been around since ancient Rome, while tomatoes, which are "new world" foods, only arrived in Europe after Europeans "discovered" the Americas. Is it possible to determine whether Esposito really was the first person to flavor bread with those particular toppings? Does it matter that there are records of "pizzas" being made in Italy (and not by Esposito) prior to 1889? Tracing the origins of a relatively recent invention like pizza is a complicated business but what about more generic foods like bread, soup or, indeed, salad?

Tradition and Innovation

A friend of mine once told me about the time she tried to recreate her mother's pot roast recipe. For years, her mother had cooked her roast in a particular way, and a key step involved cutting off the ends of the roast before putting it in the oven. But when my friend triumphantly placed her version of the roast on the table, her mother was baffled by the cut ends. When my friend explained that she had cut the ends because that's what her mother did, her mother explained she had only ever done that because her roasting pan was too small!

Actually, I have no idea where that story comes from. For years I thought a friend really did tell me about her pot roast and mother, but a quick internet search revealed the story is a common one with many variations (Mikkelson 1999). The point of the story is that traditions ought to be questioned and that what is traditional is not always best. Yet "traditional" often becomes synonymous with both "best" and "authentic," and claims that food is made in the "traditional way" provide that food with an air of authenticity and quality. Consider whipped cream. The earliest written recipes dating from the 17th century instruct chefs to whip cream chilled over ice with a willow branch. The wire whisk was invented in the 19th century, and artificial refrigeration only became common in homes by the middle of the 20th century. While contemporary chefs might argue over whether to use a hand whisk or stand mixer for preparing whipped cream, as far as I know no one argues "traditional" willow branches are best or that cream should only ever be cooled using ice (Larson 2020).

Hyper-Reality and Hyper-Authentic Realms

We live in a world in which digital transmission and reproduction are commonplace. For many of us, our first encounter with any given apparent original occurs online (the Wikipedia article on the *Mona Lisa* vs. the actual painting in the Louvre, for instance). Given the representational complexity of our (post)modern world, a number of writers and thinkers have questioned whether apparently clear-cut distinctions such as authentic vs. inauthentic or real vs. unreal continue to be either meaningful or possible.

The term "hyperreal" was coined by the French philosopher Jean Baudrillard. In his book *Simulacra and Simulation,* Baudrillard defines the hyperreal as "the generation ... of a real without origin or reality..." (Baudrillard 1994: 1). In Baudrillard's use, the prefix "hyper" means "beyond" rather than "extremely." Baudrillard discusses Disneyland, but The Wizarding World of Harry Potter (WWHP) theme parks are perhaps even better examples of hyperreality at work. Fans of the Harry Potter series who visit a WWHP theme park expect to see and interact with familiar scenes from the books or films *in real life*. Visitors can board a functioning Hogwarts Express™ and walk the streets of a real, live Hogsmeade™ Village. Yet these real-life experiences and objects are not forgeries of pre-existing realities: they are authentic representations of imaginary realms whose origins lie—not in the world—but in the minds of author J. K. Rowling and the various directors of the film franchise. In situations like this one, what sense does it make to distinguish between authentic and inauthentic experiences? Given that *butterbeer* is a *fictional* drink, how can the authenticity of a given recipe ever be adjudicated (Krishna 2017).

I visited Walt Disney World with my sister as a child and we collected autographs from familiar Disney characters. When we were unable to get Mickey Mouse's autograph, my sister forged it. Given

28 *Fabricating Authenticity*

that the authentic autograph would have been that of a *cartoon character* (as drawn by a person wearing an authorized costume in a theme park in Florida), does it make any sense to call my sister's version a fake? Yes and no. In such instances, which are becoming ever more common given the blurred lines between fiction and reality we currently face, apparently clear-cut distinctions between real and fake become increasingly fuzzy.

Authenticity tends to be presented as a binary: something either is or isn't authentic. But the examples I've described and McCutcheon's quest for authentic Greek food reveal that authenticity is perhaps best thought of as a spectrum. The complicating factor is that whether or not something is authentic depends less on the thing itself and more on the (necessarily subjective) expectations of the various persons involved. Authenticity is not, therefore, a quality that adheres to an object but is a social accomplishment produced by the interaction of various self-interested actors, each with their own idiosyncratic preferences—for pine nuts, say (Guptill et al. 2017: 38).

Ian Alexander Cuthbertson is an independent scholar who is broadly interested in exploring how the category "religion" is deployed to legitimize certain beliefs, practices, and institutions while delegitimizing others. Ian lives in England with his wife Virginia and their son Ciaran and often puts pineapple on pizza.

References

Baudrillard, Jean (1994). *Simulacra and Simulation*, trans. Sheila Faria Glaser. Ann Arbor, MI: University of Michigan Press.

Fried, Andrew, dir. (2018). *Chef's Table*. Season 5, episode 3, "Bo Songvisava." Aired 28 September 2018, Netflix.

Guptill, Amy Elizabeth, Denise A. Copelton, and Betsy Lucal (2017). *Food & Society: Principles and Paradoxes*, 2nd edition. Cambridge, MA: Polity Press.

Krishna, Priya (2017). "The Man Who Holds the Top Secret Recipe for Butterbeer." *Bon Appétit*. 30 May. Retrieved from https://www. bonappetit.com/story/butterbeer-recipe-wizarding-world-of-harry-potter (accessed 27 August 2020).

Larson, Sarah (2020). "When To Use A Mixer and When To Use Your Hands." *Escoffier*. 20 July. Retrieved from https://www.escoffier.edu/blog/baking-pastry/when-to-use-a-mixer-and-when-to-use-your-hands/ (accessed 27 August 2020).

Mikkelson, Barbara (1999). "Grandma's Cooking Secret." *Snopes.com*. 9 November. Retrieved from https://www.snopes.com/fact-check/grandmas-cooking-secret/ (accessed 27 August 2020).

3. Marketing the Authentic Taco

Jason W. M. Ellsworth

As I drive across my home province of Prince Edward Island (PEI) in Canada looking for a place to eat lunch, I feel overwhelmed by advertising that offers what seems to be an endless array of food options. Do I want fresh and healthy or fast and fried? How about seafood, pizza, burgers, or wings? Or vegetarian, vegan, gluten free, local, GMO-free, keto, or organic? Maybe something from an all you can eat Chinese buffet, fine Italian dining, "exotic flavors" from an Indian restaurant or maybe an Irish alehouse.

Even in the small capital city of Charlottetown (population of ~ 36,000) my options seem endless, a potential stimulating subject matter in itself on the globalization of food. However, there is one type of food that appears to be available on every street that always piques my curiosity—"authentic." One can find restaurants that promote a truly "authentic Thai food dining experience," or "genuine Northern Italian cuisine," and the "most authentic Chinese food in town." But it's not only the restaurants that promote this: an initiative known as Canada's Food Island has an entire section of their website dedicated to "Authentic PEI Products" (Canada's Food Island 2018). With so many selling it, how does one differentiate between the inauthentic and the authentic?

Take, for example, a local newspaper article where the owner of a then newly opened La Sazón de Mexico states that it is the first Mexican food restaurant in the city and claims it is the only one with "authentic Mexican food" (Stewart 2018). The owner says the restaurant aims to showcase what is "real Mexican culture" and even offers "authentic Mexican tequila." The large red sign out front has the words "Authentic Mexican Cuisine" front and center.

However, as the restaurant only recently opened, the claim to authenticity seems to challenge other existing businesses that have already made similar declarations to Mexican authenticity. Taco Boyz, another local restaurant in the same city, boasts on their website that they have been "serving up fresh, authentic Mexican food since 2014!" (Taco Boyz 2018). They claim to use "classic Mexican cooking methods," sourcing local products and offering "Mexican inspired street food" cooked using "authentic recipes in-store every day." Their logo even bares a stamp, front and center, claiming it is an "Authentic Mexican Grill."

By claiming to be the first Mexican food restaurant La Sazón de Mexico's authenticity declaration seems to be pointed directly at the existing Taco Boyz claim. So, which one really was the first "authentic" Mexican food restaurant in town?

While these two restaurants duke it out over which is more "authentic," other restaurants take another approach. On their Instagram page, Sugar Skull Cantina, a Tex-Mex cantina style taco and tequila bar, advertises "tacos without borders. Originality makes us happy, not authenticity" (Sugar Skull Cantina 2018). The notion of "originality" legitimizes a creative aspect that is somehow beyond authenticity. Yet, it still normalizes a notion that there is an "authentic" to begin with. To be original requires an opposing non-original—in this case, an inauthentic.

How, though, should one go about trying to understand these claims to authenticity? Do any of these claims point to any one specific thing or essential element that distinguishes authentic Mexican food? Or are these simply marketing tactics? According to sociologist Stephen Christ, who examined the social organization of authenticity in Mexican restaurants in the United States, while authenticity claims are highly subjective, they also act as sites for public display of ethnic and cultural identities (Christ 2015). However, he further extends on this, stating in one interview:

> The power to define something as authentic rests not with the restaurant owner but rather in the hands of mostly white, American consumers who have had little experience or knowledge of Mexican food or traditional styles of preparation. ... The owner of

32 *Fabricating Authenticity*

> a Mexican restaurant may claim to have the most authentic facility because his chef is from Mexico or he has more employees from Mexico than any of his competitors. But for the consumer, the most important consideration is "how much does this food fit my expectation of what Mexican food is based on growing up and having taco day at high school or eating at fast-food taco restaurants?" (Sossamon 2015)

While this analysis is centered in the context of the U.S., it offers but one way to approach the comparable authenticity claims made by restaurants in PEI by addressing who is given power to legitimize these very claims.

So, rather than being descriptive of a particular quality or essence, authenticity is often contestable and hard to pin down. It is frequently a mechanism for marketing, used to separate one thing from another—the real from the unreal or the us from them. But who gets to decide where the separation lies and what deserves the label of authenticity? This discourse of authenticity seems to appeal to a fetish for "real" or "genuine" experiences. And yet for some, the authenticity narrative can be a means to protect their culture from being vulgarized by outsiders who look to profit from an imagined notion of the real. Perhaps the rhetoric of authenticity tells us less about the actual food stuff that is advertised on a restaurant sign and more about those making and consuming the claim.

Jason W. M. Ellsworth is a doctoral candidate in the Sociology and Social Anthropology Department at Dalhousie University. He currently works at the Faculty of Medicine at the University of Prince Edward Island and serves on the Executive Committee of the Canadian Anthropology Society. His research explores a diverse array of topics including the Anthropology and Sociology of Religion, Buddhism in North America, Food and Food Movements, Theories of Value, Political Economy, Marketing, Transnationalism, and Orientalism.

References

Canada's Food Island (2018). "Culinary Trail: Authentic PEI Products." *Canada's Food Island.* Retrieved from https://canadasfoodisland.ca/culinary-trail/ (accessed 8 January 2020).

Christ, Stephen (2015). "The Social Organization of Authenticity in Mexican Restaurants," *Organizational Cultures: An International Journal* 15/2: 11–16. https://doi.org/10.18848/2327-8013/CGP/v15i02/50948

Sossamon, Jeff (2015). "'Authenticity' in Mexican Restaurants Depends on Views of Managers and Patrons." *University of Missouri: News Bureau,* September 2. Retrieved from https://munewsarchives.missouri.edu/news-releases/2015/0902-authenticity-in-mexican-restaurants-depends-on-views-of-managers-and-patrons/ (accessed 8 January 2020).

Stewart, Dave (2018). "New Mexican food restaurant opens in downtown Charlottetown." *SaltWire,* February 7. Retrieved from https://www.saltwire.com/prince-edward-island/business/new-mexican-food-restaurant-opens-in-downtown-charlottetown-184216/ (accessed 8 January 2020).

Sugar Skull Cantina (@sugarskullpei) (2018). *Instagram.* https://www.instagram.com/sugarskullpei/ (accessed 8 January 2020; website inactive 2024).

Taco Boys (2017). "About Taco Boyz." *Taco Boyz.* Retrieved from https://www.tacoboyz.com/about-taco-boyz/ (accessed 8 January 2020).

4. A Remembrance of Dishes Past

Rachel D. Brown

If you're anything like me, you were binging almost every show on Netflix while in isolation in 2020. Being stuck in our homes thanks to the Covid-19 pandemic led to a need for mediated escapes. Hence, I binged shows that took me to other places in the world, that showed me the kinds of vistas I wanted to be looking at, and that introduced me to the kinds of flavors I wanted to be tasting. If a show could also make me think and cause me to reflect on something that interests me academically, all the better. One of the shows that has provided me with all of the above is David Chang's *Ugly Delicious* (2018a).

When I watched Chang's first season of *Ugly Delicious* a few years ago, I picked it apart thoroughly. As a scholar of food and religion, I have a hard time watching shows that deal with either topic because I usually jump right into analysis mode and often cannot just sit back to enjoy them. I usually start saying things like "Oh come on Chang, what definition of authenticity are you even applying here?" I think that chefs and entertainers like Chang should somehow be able to engage, and even be interested in, the level of academic analysis in which I have spent years being trained, especially because *he's* the one who used the word "authenticity." Surely, he had to know that the very utterance would open him up to hefty academic critique! It's almost a Pavlovian response. The truth of the matter is shows like *Ugly Delicious* actually have a way of getting at the heart of a question, in this case of "authenticity," in ways that may be more interesting, grounded, and nuanced than most academics I know. As I watched the second season, with a seemingly more mature, humble, and inquisitive Chang, I found myself asking, "if David Chang can deal effectively and impressively with the discourse of authenticity and food, what role is there left for us, as scholars of this topic, to do?"

The debate around "authenticity" abounds all throughout *Ugly Delicious*. Chang even opens the first episode by saying: "I view authenticity like a totalitarian state… It's not that I hate authenticity, it's that I hate that people want this singular thing that is authentic" (Chang 2018b). Interestingly enough, while Season 1 addresses "authenticity" head on, I think the real work of critiquing, dissecting, and pulling apart the discourse of "authenticity" happens in Season 2. All without directly engaging with it. As Jenny Zhang suggests in her review of the show, while Season 1 is about the "questioning of culinary 'authenticity,'" Season 2 is more about "Chang owning up to what he doesn't know" (Zhang 2020). It's in this owning up to what he doesn't know and consequently relying heavily on the explorations and explanations of others (such as chefs, celebrities, scholars, journalists, and home cooks) that some thoughtful insights about "authenticity" arise.

First, as Jason W. M. Ellsworth notes in his chapter, building on an example from Stephen Christ, it is not only business owners' and chefs' claims that need analysis, but also consumers often play an active role in the process; thus their power to legitimize and evaluate claims to authenticity is particularly important to recognize. As Chang opens Episode 2 of his second season he talks, in his infamous bad boy kind of way, about the fact that what is "authentic" is determined by the consumer walking into a given restaurant and ordering "what in *their* world, comprises a Korean [or any other ethnic food] menu, because they don't know what the fuck they're doing." Here one assumes that Chang is expanding on his fear, and related critique, from season one that "only a white face can make a food authentic" (Herapocrypha 2018). In fact, much of Season 1 is about Chang's fear that non-Korean consumers (usually white Americans) may be the ones to determine what he should, or what he needs, to prepare in his restaurants in order to be labeled as "authentic" and therefore successful in the American restaurant world. If Chang had left his comment there, critiquing the many people who pretend that they know what "authentic" such and such food is, one could argue that this

36   *Fabricating Authenticity*

episode could easily be placed in the rather uninteresting approach of Season 1. But Chang doesn't leave it there. Instead, he goes on and finishes his sentence by saying, "I'm that asshole when I go to an Indian restaurant" (2018a). He turns his critique upon himself and shows how he feeds into the idea of the construction of "authenticity" by so called "outsiders." While on the one hand, he feels he has a right to determine "authenticity" as a cook (of Korean food), he has to acknowledge that he is also a consumer who participates in the construction of the "authentic" without the kind of connection to the "real" that he seems to emphasize is necessary.

This leads to another aspect of the discourse of "authenticity" that is dealt with in *Ugly Delicious*: that by making "authenticity" claims, or even by claiming one is not interested in "authenticity," it all "still normalizes a notion that there is an 'authentic' to begin with" (Ellsworth, Chapter 3). While in Season 1 the constant engagement with the idea of "authenticity" continually reifies the idea that there is some *sine qua non* that is "real," "true," "unaltered" pizza, tacos, or fried chicken for example, in Season 2 things get a lot more murky, confusing even. Although there are episodes about curry, steak, and spit roasted meat, they all work hard to push back at the idea that there is any one thing that could be called any of the above, let alone an "authentic" version of it. Curry might be the example par excellence of how one cannot hope to find the "authentic" version because the variations of dishes that people refer to as "curry" are so vast and varied that it comes across as an absolute absurdity to even think one could go on the hunt for it. Episode 4, on Middle Eastern food, emphasizes this point. In all of this, Chang somehow gets the viewer to think about what "authenticity" means, and whether it's even possible, without even using the word and he does so more effectively than I often do in my university classes.

But, in an attempt to try and not write myself out of a job, I will say that there are a few important aspects of the conversation around "authenticity" and food that I think Chang misses. For the sake of space, I will focus on one quick example: memory. As Herapocrypha argues, "Chang is trying to figure out the mechanics of *how* to preserve and build upon the authentic," and "*How* exists in the remembrance of home food, of a person, typically a mother or auntie or grandma, cooking either from memory or a mixture of memory and necessity, with varying levels of emotional investment" (2020). Many, Chang included, will suggest that the memory of a place/dish provides grounding for what is "authentic," and the argument is often that one must have direct memory, or access to someone with direct memory, in order to produce "authentic" food. This perspective seems to give memory a characteristic of infallibility though. Anthropologist Simon Coleman suggests that ethnographers are often "concerned with how to translate an 'authentic' sense of 'being there' to the reader, we can also add that ethnographies also contain tensions linked to how 'being *then*' can be worked into a text that may be written many years later" (2010: 215). One could replace "ethnographer" with "cook" and see how cooks, when caught up in the performance of authenticity (whether by their own interest or because consumers force them into the performance), attempt to translate "being there" and "being then" to the consumer of their food. The problem is that memory is flawed. If cooks are anything like ethnographers, the remembrance of a place, time, dish, is often imperfect, and usually impacted by various positionalities that the ethnographer/cook brings to the remembering process. One may ask then, can the "authentic" ever exist if one can never fully lock down the original—or better—"authentic" memory? Is the best we can hope for just an appreciation for really good food and the ways that really good food can help to break down walls between people (as Chang suggests in Season 2, Episode 4)?

So, who gets to determine and discuss what is "authentic"? Is it the scholar, the cook, or the consumer? Interestingly enough, one can apply similar questions, concerns, and perspectives to thinking about one of my main interests—religion. What is "authentic" religion and who gets to decide? Is it the cook (religious founder, leader, text writer, etc.), the consumer (religious adherents, practitioners, dabblers, etc.), or the scholar (many of us sitting in our offices, twice removed from the kitchen—as it were)? If Chang's work on *Ugly Delicious* reveals anything, it's that we all have a stake (or steak) in the game and sometimes the tastiest revelations and reflections come from the place we might least expect; so, it's probably best to ask, and listen to, everyone to determine just what type of work is being done with these discourses. Even then, as Chang says, we're all simply

38   *Fabricating Authenticity*

ignorant assholes, so why not just throw out the word "authenticity" all together, and just go get some tacos because they taste good, not because they are "authentic." Though we might need to remember that what "tastes good" is socially, relationally, culturally, and politically determined largely by our class or habitus, though perhaps that's something to contend with at another meal.

Rachel D. Brown is the Program & Research Coordinator at the Centre for Studies in Religion and Society, and an Assistant Teaching Professor in Anthropology and Religion, Culture, and Society, at the University of Victoria in British Columbia, Canada. She has a Ph.D. in Religion and Culture from Wilfrid Laurier University and specializes in food, migration, lived religion, and contemporary Islam. Rachel has published multiple journal articles and book chapters on food and migration/minorities, Muslim integration in France, the experience of minority religious communities in the Pacific Northwest, and researcher positionality and knowledge production.

References

Chang, David, creator (2018a). *Ugly Delicious*. Tremolo Productions. Netflix.

———. (2018b). *Ugly Delicious*. Season 1, episode 1, "Pizza." Aired 23 February 2018, Netflix.

Coleman, Simon (2010). "On Remembering and Forgetting in Writing and Fieldwork." In Peter Collins and Anselma Gallinat (eds.), *The Ethnographic Self as Resource: Writing Memory and Experience into Ethnography*, 215–222. New York: Berghahn Books. https://doi.org/10.1515/9781845458287-014

Herapocrypha (2018). "Chang's Madeleine: 'Ugly Delicious' and the Problem of Authenticity." *Medium*, 18 April. Retrieved from https://medium.com/@N.A.Stanley/changs-madeleine-ugly-delicious-and-the-problem-of-authenticity-83c7e5d9c05b (accessed 30 August 2020).

Zhang, Jenny G. (2020). "A Humbler, More Vulnerable David Chang Emerges in 'Ugly Delicious' Season 2." *Eater*, 6 March. Retrieved from https://www.eater.com/2020/3/6/21166944/david-chang-ugly-delicious-season-2-netflix-review (accessed 30 August 2020).

5. Because YOU'RE an Early Adopter (and I'M NOT): Commodity Fetishism and Identification

Christopher R. Cotter

In mid-2018, my regular walks to and from my local gym in Edinburgh took me past a bus shelter displaying an advertisement for two new flavors of Diet Coke—"Feisty Cherry" and "Exotic Mango." The tagline presented alongside the minimalist photograph of the two cans of Diet Coke on a plain white background simply read "because you're an early adopter." This exhortation—implicitly citing Everett M. Rogers' (2003) academic development of the adopter typology— coupled with my then recent first viewing of *Mad Men* prompted the following reflections on how various elements of boundaries, branding, and consumerism are linked to, establish, and complicate constructions of the "true" and "authentic" self.

Setting aside the fact that Cherry Coke was introduced in 1985, and the lack of clarity surrounding what makes this variant more "feisty" than what came before—indeed, there is a notable lack of *any* information about the product—the central message here is that the specifics of the product do not matter. What matters is that YOU should purchase it because YOU are a trend-setter. It is an aspirational message, spoken to a stereotyped millennial Instagrammer:

> YOUR patterns of consumption are so much more on point than others, who admire YOU so much they'll want to emulate YOU. We, YOUR friends at Coca-Cola, want YOU to be a key element in the dissemination of this product. Because YOU are special.

40   *Fabricating Authenticity*

> Because YOU have a valuable ability to recognize what will be popular before it's popular. Because YOU are an early adopter.

After all, what could be worse than being a sheep following the rest of the herd? This imagined consumer is the sheep who is out in front. YOU are not just *any* sheep, but the *leader* of the sheep. But a sheep is still a sheep, right?

This is an excellent example of what Karl Marx deemed "commodity fetishism," whereby the market exchange of commodities, and the value placed upon them as objects by apparently autonomous rational actors, obscures the underlying economic character of the relationship of production between the worker and those with economic power. Marx finds an analogy in "the misty realm of religion" where "products of the human brain appear as autonomous figures endowed with a life of their own, which enter into relations both with each other and with the human race" (1990: 165). In critical religious studies (e.g., Fitzgerald 2015; Hughes 2015), this process is known as reification: the "apprehension of the products of human activity"—here, the category "religion" itself—"as if they were something else than human products" (Berger and Luckmann 1966: 89). In Marx's economic theory, the analogous process of fetishism results in commodities being constructed as having *sui generis* value, rather than as the products of "definite social relation[s] between men [*sic*] themselves" (Marx 1990: 165). Thus, this renders the exchange of commodities as an interaction between consumer and (intrinsically valuable) commodity, rather than between consumer and the vast (and, for Marx, unjust) economic system that has produced, marketed and imparted value upon said commodity.

Because the lines of production and marketing are obscured through commodity fetishism, consumers are constructed as individual rational actors making autonomous authentic choices based upon real or authentic relationships with the commodities they encounter. Because commodities are constructed as things with intrinsic value in-and-of themselves, one's commodity choices come to be seen as unique aspects of one's identity, rather than as "operational acts of identification" (Bayart 2005: 92). We see the same rhetoric in vernacular assertions—from all sides of the "debate"—that a person's religious "identity" is a choice, or that authentic religious adherents are those who have thought about their position, and explicitly and rationally adopted it. This is essentially the perspective of Rational Choice Theory (Stark and Bainbridge 1987; Stark and Finke 2000) which arguably over-emphasizes the autonomy of the individual. Rather than seeing the individual as an authentic, coherent whole making rational decisions, I—along with Bayart and the contributors to this volume—argue that (religious) identification, purchasing decisions, and other operational acts are characterized by "indeterminism, incompletion, multiplicity and polyvalence" (Bayart 2005: 109), and are heavily influenced by "the communities and cultures with which we have relations" (ibid.: 95).

Returning to the advert at focus, what makes this an even more impressive example of commodity fetishism is that it attempts to gain the trust of the viewer by letting them in on its manipulative intent. In a manner akin to the "Mr. Charles" gambit in Christopher Nolan's *Inception* (2010), where Leonardo DiCaprio's thief slyly reveals to Cillian Murphy's businessman that he is dreaming in order to gain his trust and further manipulate his subconscious, the advert informs the viewer of its manipulative intent. It is effectively saying: "Most consumers of this product are going to make inauthentic, manipulated choices—but YOU can make an authentic one!" But just how authentic can a choice be, when one has just been manipulated by a powerhouse international corporation?

In my day-to-day life, I tend to take great pleasure in rattling off versions of this critique, railing against the (type of) capitalism instantiated in this advertisement. "I don't follow trends," I say. "I don't buy things just because they are—or might become—fads. I wait until the price comes down, until there are a few years of feedback, until the technology has become so ubiquitous that the premium for the 'new' is removed." Because "my time is so precious and important," I "don't have time to watch the latest things on television," and thus I consume *Mad Men* when I want to. *When I have made an authentic decision.*

All of this is exemplary of my participation in a particular discourse. A discourse in which I, the academic who can write chapters about commodity fetishism, am supposedly "better" than "everyone

42   *Fabricating Authenticity*

else," the "unthinking masses" who seemingly follow the directives of corporations; who apparently feel compelled to enjoy the same entertainment as their contemporaries at the same time because of #FOMO; who simply must own the latest piece of technology, dress in the most fashionable of styles, know all the latest gossip, and be known to be listening to the latest music as if their lives depended on it. In short, I am the stereotypical, holier-than-thou academic.

By participating in this discourse, I construct an autonomous-authentic self that allows me to feel comfortable as I move about the world. It has been built up over years of feeling unable to keep abreast of every issue, feeling behind the curve, and never being one of the cool kids. And this has then been compounded over the past decade by my identification as part of the imagined community of "academics." There are alternative discourses: I could be deemed "unfashionable," "out of touch," "irrelevant," "uncool," "sad," and "dull." And my imagined community of opponents, the "early adopters," might well see themselves as "ahead of the trend," "fashionable," "up-to-date," "relevant," "peak," "sick," "chic," "fun," "vibrant," "in touch," and so on. My point? There is nothing inherently "true" in either of these dichotomous discourses. Ultimately, why is Shakespeare more "proper" than *Love Island*? Why is fashion a "lesser" form of art than "high art"? Why is my consumption of academic texts, *Star Trek*, Stella Artois and 0% fat natural yoghurt any more or less problematic/edificatory than someone else's consumption of caviar, Oprah Winfrey, *Vogue* or McDonald's? It's all a question of power and boundary maintenance, and the construction of that imagined community and an "authentic" self.

In *The Pervert's Guide to Ideology*, Slavoj Žižek discusses John Carpenter's dystopian science-fiction film *They Live* (1988), in which a man finds a box of mysterious sunglasses which enable him to see the ideological messages encoded in the material world around him. Here, Žižek uses this example to argue that "the tragedy of our predicament when we are within ideology is that when we think that we escape it—into our dreams—at that point we are within ideology" (Fiennes 2012). By letting the imagined consumer in on the manipulation—by encouraging the notion that the consumer's choice is genuine and authentic—the advertisers at focus in this chapter maintain,

COTTER *Because YOU'RE an Early Adopter (and I'M NOT)* 43

and reinforce, their ideological grip. At the same time, I—the academic writing about commodity fetishism—think that I have escaped the manipulation to a point of objective authenticity, yet I am just as much a pawn as the "early adopter." I can't help but recall a similar point that Timothy Fitzgerald made about academics studying "religion" in his *The Ideology of Religious Studies*:

> The industry known as religious studies is a kind of generating plant for a value laden view the world that claims to identify religions and faiths as an aspect of all societies and that, by so doing, makes possible another separate "non-religious" conceptual space, a fundamental area of presumed factual objectivity. (2000: 8)

In any case, no matter what I think, I am an "early adopter." Because I have consumed Diet Coke for as long as I can remember. I can't abide "normal" Coca-Cola. And Pepsi just isn't the same. And realistically these are my only two options, right? So, all that work was done years ago, before I can even remember. But if I am an early adopter, at least I can take comfort in being an authentic one...

Christopher R. Cotter is lecturer in Religious Studies and Sociology at the Open University. He is co-founder *of The Religious Studies Project*, author of *The Critical Study of Non-Religion: Discourse, Identification, Locality* (Bloomsbury, 2020), and co-editor of *After World Religions: Reconstructing Religious Studies* (Routledge, 2016).

References

Bayart, Jean-François (2005). *The Illusion of Cultural Identity*. London: C Hurst & Co Publishers Ltd.

Berger, Peter, and Thomas Luckmann (1966). *The Social Construction of Reality: A Treatise in the Sociology of Knowledge*. Garden City: Anchor Books.

Carpenter, John, dir. (1988). *They Live*. Universal Pictures.

Fiennes, Sophie, dir. (2012). *The Pervert's Guide to Ideology*. P Guide Productions / Zeitgeist Films.

44 Fabricating Authenticity

Fitzgerald, Timothy (2000). *The Ideology of Religious Studies*. New York and Oxford: Oxford University Press.

———. (2015). "Negative Liberty, Liberal Faith Postulates, and World Disorder." In Trevor Stack, Naomi R. Goldenberg, and Timothy Fitzgerald (eds.), *Religion as a Category of Governance and Sovereignty*, 248–279. Leiden and Boston: Brill. https://doi.org/10.1163/9789004290594_012

Hughes, Aaron W. (2015). *Islam and the Tyranny of Authenticity: An Inquiry into Disciplinary Apologetics and Self-Deception*. Sheffield, UK: Equinox Publishing Ltd.

Marx, Karl (1990). *Capital: Critique of Political Economy*. London: Penguin Classics.

Nolan, Christopher, dir. (2010). *Inception*. Warner Bros.

Rogers, Everett M. (2003). *Diffusion of Innovations*, 5th ed. New York: Free Press.

Stark, Rodney, and Roger Finke (2000). *Acts of Faith: Explaining the Human Side of Religion*. Berkeley, CA: University of California Press.

Stark, Rodney, and William Sims Bainbridge (1987). *A Theory of Religion*. New York: Peter Lang.

6. Fool's Gold: Tapping into Luxury

Ping-hsiu Alice Lin

Shopping malls of the twenty-first century evoke a sense of unease in me—and not only because of the COVID-19 pandemic. Looking through large glass windows showcasing what I often feel are unprepossessing objects, all I can think of is the excess of monetary value these products generate, of a triumphant capitalism that lines the pockets and enriches the lives of a miniscule number of haves. As a "90s kid," I'm familiar with the aesthetics of departmental stores where my parents, and later I, would spend hours shopping for things that we felt we, however momentarily, desired or needed. The shopping centers of my childhood were, as cultural theorist Meaghan Morris described, "minimally readable" in that they alternated between fostering a broad sense of familiarity and surprise (Morris 1998). As sites of consumption, the mall's spatial layout, décor, festivities, and merchandise play an important role in how visitors experience their consumption practices, whether sensorially, perceptively, or emotionally. Moving to a sequence of metropolises for graduate study meant stepping into concrete landscapes further dominated by commercial centers—except they didn't necessarily inspire a sense of familiarity. Instead, malls and their paraphernalia increasingly compete for a compelling vision of luxury, horizontally and vertically. The uneven but spectacular rise in purchasing power of a growing consumerist middle class across urban centers in the Global North and South has, in tandem with ever-expanding industrialization, rapidly changed the aesthetics of shopping malls and markets.

Like the Parisian Haussmann architecture discussed in Walter Benjamin's seminal work *The Arcades Project* (2002), where

46   *Fabricating Authenticity*

activities of consumption become an aesthetic experience by virtue of the design of the arcade—a succession of contiguous arches—late modern aesthetic shopping spaces place consumerist practices symbolically and geographically at the center, rather than the margins of a space, in ways that I argue, reinsert the "authentic."

My observations here focus on Hong Kong, where I pursued my degree in anthropology, and which is a place where urban space is replete with multi-story shopping malls full of flagship stores and concept boutiques. These malls are often connected to each other through air-conditioned walkways and flyovers. Away from Hong Kong's street-level clutter and density, these exclusive spaces prominently display names like Tiffany & Co., Hermes, and Piaget. Their iconic and colossal architectural designs sell a range of items that may not qualify as universal necessities but are uniformly expensive and highly desired. From jewelry embedded with precious stones to bags likened to architectural art and gold watches, the sensory aspect of it all is best summarized by the term "luxury," a conceptual product of the collective pursuit of authenticity that is constructed on unstable grounds.

There is no precise definition of the label "luxury" because it is fluid and constantly changing. The bulk of its contemporary usage is unreflective of its social and cultural implications. Luxury and its associated products are characterized not by necessity but by desirability and qualitative finesse; luxury is thus a relative concept, shaped by cultural specificities and time periods. The luxury goods industry that includes the brands I name above once dominated major markets in Europe and North America; now, these brands have also found a formidable clientele in East Asia, where these metropolitan cities appear to be planned around shopping and tourism.

Since I began my dissertation project on the supply chain of a luxury commodity—precious stones—I've found an endless source of wonderment and alienation in documenting the ways in which people talk about some of the most luxurious commodities in the world. In the month of April 2017, I was forwarded a short promotional video on WhatsApp. Sotheby's, one of the world's largest London-based auction houses, had set a new world record by selling one of the most expensive gems in the world. According to the voice-over, the piece was a "59.60-carat oval mixed-cut Fancy Vivid Pink Internally Flawless diamond," acquired by a renowned jeweler in Hong Kong through a telephone bid of HK$553 million (US$71.2 M). Once the shock of hearing such an exorbitant price had faded, I could not help but reflect on the ideological significance of the item sold. One question burned brightest of all: What makes these labels—fancy, vivid, internally flawless—worth millions of dollars for a piece of compressed carbon?

More than a hundred years ago, economist and sociologist Thorstein Veblen (2005) coined the term "conspicuous consumption" to describe the tendency of the leisure class—members of the top business and landowning families in the United States or in Europe—to purchase and exhibit expensive goods. Here the term "conspicuous" denotes not something that is easily seen or visible in an outstanding way as the dictionary indicates, but consumer behavior that is unproductive, wasteful, and often unnecessary. Luxury consumption became spectacularly wasteful as capitalism evolved at the turn of the 20th century. Anthropologists have long recognized that consumption and identity-formation (or identification, following Bayart) are closely intertwined (Appadurai 1988; Miller 2001; Douglas 2014). Many analyses tend to emphasize the symbolic properties of what we buy, pointing to a "language" that communicates specific cultural meanings that we share with other members of our community. Following sociologist Pierre Bourdieu (1984), if we are to understand why people consume the things they do, we should think of consumption as "a struggle of symbols" that generates differences and distinctions between members of society. Buying luxury goods indexes signs of affluence and wealth in ways that place the owner in a separate class from others. Rather than fixate on what people *say* about the meanings of these products, one should look at what they *do* with it and how they construct concepts of the self and their world. This is perhaps why Arjun Appadurai defines "luxuries" as a special register of consumption (1988: 86).

Today, conspicuous consumption is largely tied to luxury products, things we buy that are differentiated from others by their associations with timelessness and refinement—rather than utility—and are highly desired for whatever aesthetic and sensory enjoyment they

48   *Fabricating Authenticity*

may bring to those who can afford them. As things perceived to have greater value than others, they are widely understood as symbols of the upper class and the elite and serve as an index for the evolution of capitalism itself. In this light, luxury becomes in itself a form of language. To understand luxury as a system of meanings, is to say the act of buying a luxury good is performative—something that is learned, shared, and expressed through embodied action. It is widely acknowledged, for example, that consuming caviar is luxurious. The same could be said of carrying a Louis Vuitton bag, or of wearing a sapphire jewelry set. Yet, knowledge of the semiotic meaning of these goods is also constantly in transit, as they move from one place to another in an increasingly interconnected economy.

How have so many come to fetishize objects in seemingly similar fashions from different parts of the world? Many academics have become preoccupied with grasping the cultural logic behind such consumption in an increasingly globalized world. Yet unlike marketing experts, academics argue that almost everything can move into the category of luxury, not merely things of supposed rarity or qualitative value. It is, after all, humans who give these meanings to objects in a specific context, and they are the ones who can also remove those meanings. Authenticity, therefore, manifests as much in the language of marketing luxury as in the act of purchasing it.

Now let us return to the superfluousness of the object auctioned by Sotheby's. Here I am closer to Chris Cotter's argument that the value attributed to luxuries is a case in point of Marx's commodity fetishism, whereby the idea of value pivots on the *perceived* distinctive properties of the end product, an "XYZ" kind of diamond, or a "so-and-so forth" brand of a watch. These properties, if we are to follow symbolic theorists, are sociologically interrelated to the individuals who consume them. The project of identity-making is something upon which, from individuals to unified communities, middle-class families, Bollywood films, transnational religious groups, and corporate marketers overwhelmingly converge. But is this why we build a world of luxury around us? Beyond fetishism and meaning-making, what actually motivates people to spend so much money on things? Can we politicize the idea of consuming and producing luxury?

(What, then, is the connection between commodity fetishism and meaning making?)

In the preceding chapter, Cotter notes that we all participate in the same discourse and identity construction in our consumption choices, whether we are equipped with the tools of critical thinking or not (Chapter 5). The attempt to only describe the cultural logic behind the consumption of luxury products is a tempting one, and possibly useful for marketing, but if we dig a bit deeper, the whole phenomenon of consuming luxury as a collective pursuit/act reveals itself as a rather complex interaction of symbolic, material and social paths of wealth acquisition. Both the buyer of the diamond, as well as many others who have created or acquired things of enormous value such as famous art, antiques, or stocks, are consuming legitimate cultural goods, as well as competing for rare goods. There is more that is involved here than what Veblen qualifies as conspicuous consumption or Bourdieu's social distinction; although these are clearly both at work.

I argue that luxury, just like the notion of authenticity, cannot be understood independently of material factors, social stratification, or historical change. To understand consuming luxury as solely a kind of language or ritual that has material and symbolic consequences (Douglas and Isherwood 2002) excludes the social reality and histories in which these symbolic representations come to being. As a commodity, the object (diamond or otherwise) is invested with functional and symbolic meaning, as well as a monetary character. The relative autonomy of symbols that happens in fetishism or social distinction serves to obscure processes through which the object has taken shape under unequal exchanges and modes of production. It also elides the structures of our economic system under which the accumulation and pursuit of cultural (and economic) capital constitutes more than a lifestyle or choice: our commerce-oriented society depends upon our superfluous spending habits to sustain a capitalist system. The changing landscapes of shopping malls are but one manifestation of the creeping commercialization of our—conscious or not—identity formation. So, the next time you find yourself spending far too much time shopping in a mall or too much money on a purse or jewelry, you

50 *Fabricating Authenticity*

might think a little more deeply about what it is that you are consuming and at what cost and to whom.

Ping-hsiu Alice Lin (PhD CUHK) is a sociocultural anthropologist with interests in commodities, labor and artisanship, geosciences, and extractive industries in South and Southeast Asia. Her in-progress manuscript examines the ways in which movement, labor, and imperial histories transform minerals into precious stones in the borderlands of Pakistan and Afghanistan, demonstrating how ideas related to value in minerals circulate among trade hubs in Asia. Lin is currently a postdoctoral fellow in the Anthropology Department at Harvard University. In July 2025, she will start as an assistant professor in the department. Between 2021 and 2023 she was a postdoctoral fellow at the Harvard Academy for International and Area Studies.

References

Appadurai, Arjun (ed.) (1988). *The Social Life of Things: Commodities in Cultural Perspective*. Cambridge: Cambridge University Press.

Benjamin, Walter (2002). *The Arcades Project*, trans. Howard Eiland and Kevin McLaughlin. Cambridge, MA: Harvard University Press.

Bourdieu, Pierre (1984). *Distinction: A Social Critique of the Judgement of Taste*. Cambridge, MA: Harvard University Press.

Douglas, Mary (2014). *Food in the Social Order: Studies of Food and Festivities in Three American Communities*. London and New York: Routledge.

Douglas, Mary, and Baron Isherwood (2002). *The World of Goods: Towards an Anthropology of Consumption*. London: Routledge.

Miller, Daniel (ed.) (2001). *Consumption: Critical Concepts in the Social Sciences*, Vol. 4, *Objects, Subjects and Mediations in Consumption*. London and New York: Routledge.

Morris, Meaghan (1998). *Too Soon Too Late: History in Popular Culture*. Bloomington, IN: Indiana University Press.

Veblen, Thorstein (2005). *The Theory of the Leisure Class: An Economic Study of Institutions*. Delhi: Aakar Books.

7. "Maybe she's born with it. Maybe it's Maybelline."

Tara Baldrick-Morrone

When I was younger, I remember being told that I had to wear makeup because, well, *that's what women are supposed to do*. To be a woman, one had to wear makeup. That's why a March 2018 headline on a Tampa, Florida news channel's Twitter account caught my eye: "Wearing makeup can hinder women's leadership chances, study says" (Gross 2018). Reading this headline, I thought about the tension between these two contradictory ideas: Women are supposed to wear makeup, yet wearing makeup seemed to put women at a disadvantage to, say, get a promotion or win an election. So I did what anyone else would do: I clicked on the link to find out how my refusal to wear makeup supposedly increased my chances of being a leader.

In the study "Negative Effects of Makeup Use on Perceptions of Leadership Ability Across Two Ethnicities," Esther A. James, Shauny Jenkins, and Christopher D. Watkins examined what effect the use of makeup (termed as makeup used for a "social night out") had on the perception of women's capacity for leadership. Participants in the study judged pictures of "women of Caucasian and African ethnicity" with varying levels of makeup (James, Jenkins, and Watkins 2018: 540). The results indicated that regardless of ethnicity, makeup "used for a social night out" negatively impacts possible leadership ability (ibid.). The opening line of the WFLA piece put this another way: "A new study found if women want to be great leaders in the workplace, they'll need to put down the lipstick and go easy on the mascara" (Gross 2018).

However, what interests me here is not that someone like me might be promoted as a supervisor over the likes of the latest Revlon

52 *Fabricating Authenticity*

spokesperson; rather, I am drawn to how the presumption of authority relates to how we perceive the world around us. That is to say, since our perceptions construct our reality, then it stands to reason that they also determine who (or what) we find to be authoritative. In other words, authority is not intrinsic to a person or position. But what makes someone capable of being a leader or an authority is not exactly straightforward. Some might say that it's a person's credentials or their previous experience. From this study, though, notice that it's neither of these things that makes these women capable of occupying a role of authority—it's the way they look. But why do some physical appearances suggest that a person would be a better leader than someone else?

This is where stereotypes and implicit bias come in. In a story I heard on WBUR's *Here and Now*, Jeremy Hobson, one of the radio show's hosts, spoke with Patricia Devine, a psychology professor at University of Wisconsin-Madison, about how stereotypes and biases become ingrained in our minds, especially at a young age. This is demonstrated in a story Devine recounts about one of her own students:

> [She] was responding to an accident on campus, she went to render assistance to a student who was hit by a car. And simultaneously, another woman came to render assistance. This woman was barking commands, she was saying, "Don't move the head, call 911," and my student, who's very committed to addressing issues of sexism, looked up at her and earnestly said, "Are you a nurse?" You can imagine, the woman's not a nurse, she was a doctor.

> But the nurse response is so easily provided by her socialization experiences, our learning histories, perhaps where, when she was younger, in particular, women were more likely to be nurses than physicians ... So, it's just that quick assumption that people make that will influence how they think about others, how they treat others, and as I said, the assumptions that they make that can diminish the experience of the other, or could constrain their opportunities if you're not thinking that they're capable of doing a wide range of activities, for example. (Hobson 2018)

As Devine notes, the student's initial reaction to the responding woman reveals the way unconscious biases operate, especially when quickly assessing a situation. There does not seem to be any intention to undermine the woman's authority as a doctor. Instead, the student's own implicit bias assumed that she, a woman who responds to an emergency situation, was a nurse.

To return to the point above, in a similar manner to the student's snap judgment with the doctor, we might consider that a woman's face, whether or not she is wearing makeup, carries no intrinsic value itself. Rather, what we perceive and the value attached to that perception might reveal one's own implicit bias, a bias that takes more seriously a woman who is bare-faced in comparison to one who is wearing makeup indicative of a "social night out." The capability of leadership, of authority, rests with the person doing the assessment, not the object being assessed. That is, though a term like "natural born leader" is used to describe someone who possesses traits associated with leadership, it is more likely that our perceptions project those qualities onto the person more than they expose any inherent ability.

Tara Baldrick-Morrone is a Postdoctoral Research Associate in Critical Classical Studies at Brown University. Her current research focuses on how twentieth-century American scholars and politicians used ancient Mediterranean texts to restrict access to reproductive healthcare.

References

Gross, Lila (2018). "Wearing makeup can hinder women's leadership chances, study says." *WFLA*, 12 March. Retrieved from https://www.wfla.com/news/viral-news/ wearing-makeup-can-hinder-womens-leadership-chances-study-says/.

Hobson, Jeremy (2018). "How To Recognize and Overcome Your Biases." *WBUR*, 13 March. Retrieved from http://www.wbur.org/ hereandnow/2018/03/13/biases-racism-sexism-psychology/.

James, Esther A., Shauny Jenkins, and Christopher D. Watkins (2018). "Negative Effects of Makeup Use on Perceptions of Leadership Ability Across Two Ethnicities," *Perception* 47/5: 540–549. https://doi. org/10.1177/0301006618763263

8. Satisfaction Not Guaranteed: COVID-19, Higher Ed, and the Politics of "Experience"

Sierra L. Lawson

Tara Baldrick-Morrone's chapter addresses how assumptions of authority influence rhetorical claims and perspectives on authenticity. Their examples show how assuming parties, and the actions and inactions those parties authorize through their assumptions, are evidence of the politics of the production of perceived realities. Specifically, Baldrick-Morrone analyzes how stereotypes function in a series of moments, where a woman's physical presentation is described as influencing the perception of said woman's authenticity by her social peers. The under or over application of make-up, in particular, is a key element that informs the perceptions Baldrick-Morrone describes as bound up in a series of strategies for gatekeeping authenticity. Baldrick-Morrone's analysis of these descriptions of women shows how an observer's assumptions about the intrinsic value of a woman is often based on that observer's view of how well that woman satisfies criteria for what is systematically deemed "desirable." Whether appearing on the scene of an accident, going up for a promotion, or running for public office, it seems women—and often Black women, disproportionately—are assumed to have less authenticity as a leader based on an observer's conditioned interest in the amount of make up the woman has applied (Baldrick-Morrone, Chapter 7).

Observers may claim no intention of undermining the woman's authenticity based on her physical appearance, even while drawing their conclusions from visual observation alone. Yet, it is important to recognize how the categories used to authorize observations are not independent of the informed biases the observer is bound up in.

Following Baldrick-Morrone's argument, judgements of a woman's abilities, and their authenticity as an executor of these abilities, seems highly contingent on the "experience" of the woman as described by an observer. For, as Baldrick-Morrone's chapter nicely showcases, categories are the primary means through which humans, as social beings, make sense of observations and use them to authorize such "experiences." Thus, the examples provided by Baldrick-Morrone serve as a noteworthy site for observing the processes by which the category of "experience" is defined and redefined to authorize certain observations. Looking to other sites of negotiation over the category of "experience," it becomes clear that such rhetorical tactics are quite common or, at the very least, still relevant for thinking through current statements on "experience."

Since the move to remote teaching in the spring of 2020, following the confirmation of the arrival of COVID-19 in the United States and reported fatalities reaching upwards of a hundred and fifty thousand within a few short months, many universities released plans for reopening their campuses for the fall 2020 semester. In particular, many universities alluded to and repeatedly emphasized the category of "experience" in their statements regarding operations. It seems that there are two main ways in which universities sustained a discourse on "experience" in their public statements responding to COVID-19 during the months of June and July in 2020. First, colleges appeared to lament the disruption of the "college experience" in the spring, something they evidenced by rescheduling events we might call social rituals that mark the end of the academic year for undergraduate students—such as graduation and dorm move outs. Second, many colleges have described their commitment to providing incoming undergraduate students with the "college experience" in the fall.

These two strategies both appeal to some elusive "experience" in the interest of fostering a sense of collective, positive "experience" with the institution among students, faculty, staff, employees, sports fans, and alums. These statements identify such an "experience" by name only, solidifying a narration of it as something that is referenceable without any concrete qualification of what that is or how it is being defined by the authors. Thus, "experience" becomes an undefined yet referenceable mode of being that very well might contradict

56   *Fabricating Authenticity*

other "experiences" that individuals would otherwise employ to characterize their time spent at the institution.

Experience is a useful category. Its utility comes from being made to appear inclusive while remaining highly flexible and, thus, having immense rhetorical currency. For these institutions, the category of experience simultaneously conceals and reveals. Consider well-documented aspects of the "college experience" that are routinely left out of these college's recent public statements altogether. Omissions that, when intentionally redacted from a self-narrated institutional memory, obfuscate the often complicated and nonlinear character of the "college experience." Take, for example, the number of individuals paying off student debt despite being unable to finish their degree, or those who did receive a degree but remain unemployed. Or, perhaps, the frequency with which sexual assaults occur on university campuses. Or, if you *really* want to talk about something that's abstracted from the mass-marketed "college experience," neurodegenerative diseases resulting in permanent brain damage for former college football players who weren't contracted for a dime during their playing time. Finally, thinking of the campus I am currently an employee and student of, the fresh history of student protesters being assaulted by police officers never seems to appear in the digital material aimed at incoming students.

These instances name only a few "experiences" that rarely make it onto the self-narrated institutional record as it appears in these recent statements and broader discursive claims. Yet, these narrations of "experience" could just as well be used as markers of an authentic "college experience." The named, but undefined, category of "experience" could potentially challenge the institution's ability to identify traditions that make up its history. It is this potential for dissent that informs these institution's interests in producing such statements. By actively narrating the boundaries of what counts as an authentic "experience" worth ensuring or lamenting, rehearsed silences and concealments reify the "college experience" as a self-evident, desirable commodity.

Baldrick-Morrone's chapter analyzes how descriptions of women as having certain level of authenticity—and descriptions that often mention the use of cosmetics, in particular—expose more about the interests of the person doing the describing than any inherent quality the woman might possess. The same is true for these "college experience" as it appears in statements from institutions of higher ed in response to COVID-19. The use of the word "experience" in general public statements from colleges in the US allows those writing, promoting, and distributing such statements to conceal as much information about institutional spaces as they reveal. After all, as highlighted by the previous list of examples, the modern university system plays host to a spectrum of events which could also be essentialized as definitive of individual and collective "experiences" that make college campuses complicated zones of social contact.

Reconsidering the politics of the use of the category of "experience" is a critical exercise; it highlights the narration of authenticity as contingent upon an interested describer. It is a means for challenging the use of the category of "experience" as though it references something self-evident and beyond critique. One example of this is those women in Baldrick-Morrone's chapter who were able to intervene on behalf of their own authenticity and disrupt the descriptions provided by their respective describers. In doing so, these women challenged the informed assumptions of those describers and actively re-imagined what might be considered a legible and authentic narrative of the describer's "experience." Therefore, "experience" seems a fruitful site for one to investigate the authenticity granted to certain interested descriptions over others.

Currently, in July of 2020, we are witnessing in real time how institutions of higher ed authorize certain components of the "college experience" in the name of broader institutional choices. It seems one such choice, to reopen their campuses for face-to-face instruction despite the exponential spread of COVID-19 in the United States, will become one of these "experiences." In these times, as students and pedagogues, it might do us well to reflect on the work that the category "experience" is doing for these institutions. Like the women in Baldrick-Morrone's chapter, re-imagining what we take to be an authentic "experience" might better equip us, as patrons and employees of these institutions, in understanding how our affiliated institution's narration of itself and attendant "experiences" is directly influenced by affinities and estrangements we ourselves might not

58   *Fabricating Authenticity*

align with. For, it seems, complicity in the deaths of students, faculty, staff, and other employees will continue to be left out of self-issued statements narrating such an "experience" and the politics of its desirability.

Sierra L. Lawson is a doctoral candidate in the Religion and Culture track in the department of Religious Studies at the University of North Carolina at Chapel Hill. Lawson's work situates breastmilk as one site where we can observe transatlantic early modern Spanish Catholic interests in manufacturing an intimate relationship between race, religion, and body fluids. Critically revisiting how the emergent category of religion was produced in relation to racialized labor on both sides of the Atlantic, they center a feminist analysis of bodily fluids in early colonial Lima and Cusco that examines how maternal labor including breastfeeding was understood by inhabitants of colonial Peru.

9. A Man, A Tan, "God's Plan"

Richard Newton

In 2018, hip hop artist Aubrey "Drake" Graham revealed that the knotting of his purse strings and heartstrings were all a part of "God's Plan," the title of one of the year's most controversial music videos. The Billboard hit opens with a title card explaining, "The budget for this music video was $999,631.90. We gave it all away. Don't tell the label..." (Drake 2018). The video then precedes to show Drake appearing all over Miami giving money way. Gifts ranged from surprise shopping sprees to impromptu educational grants and scholarships to unexpected spa treatments.

The emotional reception shown in the video matched the public's initial positive reactions. Some people shown are more familiar with Drake's celebrity than others. All, however, are elated by his generosity. Tears, cheers, grins, and awe dispel the disbelief of those counting themselves fortunate to have crossed paths with the artist. At one point in the video, the music cuts out and two men can be heard talking. One says, "Say what you said again." The other replies, "Thank God for what is happening right now. It may not be good. But thank God. And I do" (ibid.). The precise context of the dialogue is unclear, but interlaced with the premise of the video, it surfaces familiar questions about the politics of explanation, social agency, and ultimately, identity.

We should be careful not to overlook why people appear so happy to receive the money. Drake's gift is appreciated by recipients because they understand themselves to be "in need." Without this context, the gesture would not likely elicit such responses. In the interlude, the man says that God should be thanked regardless of the circumstance—e.g., "what is happening right now. It may not be good" (ibid.). While this sort of attribution is not strange to me as a student of religion, its appearance here made me more aware of how

60   *Fabricating Authenticity*

explanations function socially. The statement isn't about causality so much as it is supremacy. Being near or an extension of that prime mover (as Drake seems to be here) is an awesome political move. How often are explanations opportunities to shore up social capital (Bourdieu 1986)?

This is part of what makes Drake's philanthropy so intriguing. It mystifies the exchange represented in the media. He gives money away as part of a music video meant to draw audience attention, leading to increased interest and profits associated with his art. This would be mundane were we to replace "gives money away as…" with "spends money on…" Yet the act of giving changes how we identify the dynamics at play. To put it plainly, spending money to make money is a cultural norm, but there's something edgy about giving away that money to make money.

The issue is not about financial expense but the undisclosed work that goes into the act. Thus, the occasion of Drake's philanthropy has since been subject to a variety of interpretations. Was this all a publicity stunt? Shouldn't he have given his money through proper charitable channels? Wouldn't that money be better spent on structural issues? A journalist asked me to weigh in on these queries as part of his research into Drake's "God's Plan" (Cornelius 2018). As a scholar of religion, I suggest that many of the social movements that people identify as worthwhile are associated with conspicuous public giving. Philosophers, ethicists, and theologians are not wrong in noting the appeal of, say, those gospel admonitions about doing good works in secret. We would also do well to consider the politics of such admonitions. The idea of a gospel (i.e., good news) is to publicize good works after all.

What is so compelling about altruism when self-interests are often—if not, always—part of the equation? Not five minutes after the phone interview on "God's Plan" did I drive by a church sign exemplifying the point. The marquee said, "Love is so nice to receive, but far more to give." And just below this sentence was a small, standard announcement of the church's 11 a.m. worship service. If the question is about biblical virtue, which is more "genuine," public giving that inspires people to do likewise or keeping one's deeds secret? Defining which is more authentic is not the question I'm keen on answering here. I am interested in why everybody's a critic when we discuss philanthropy but not all peoples' benevolence is subjected to the same critique.

For instance, pop-punk band Blink-182 had a 2001 music video for the song, "The Rock Show," featuring the group giving away their $500,000 production allotment. Their spending was not as conventionally wholesome as Drake's. Lead singer Travis Barker explained, "We took all the money they gave us for the video, and instead of renting sports cars and getting a bunch of stupid dancers, we spent the money destroying things and being weird" (Puckett 2018). In addition to giving cash to people in Los Angeles, they purchased objects to destroy, visited a strip club, and hosted pop-up concerts and skate shows. It was a display of rock and roll living at its finest. Meanwhile Drake presents a video—against the oft-maligned extravagance of many hip-hop videos—and receives a mixed review. What makes Drake so different? That's the question.

Business mogul Shawn Carter (aka Jay-Z) may be onto something in a verse from "Murder to Excellence." His signification on the Protestant work ethic leads me to wonder whether an evaluation of giving can be separated from our read of the people doling out the money.

> I stink of success, the new Black elite.
> They say my Black Card bears the mark of the beast.
> I repeat: my religion is the beat.
> My verse is like church, my Jesus piece.
> (Jay-Z and Kanye West 2011)

Anointing becomes a stench when the person paying fortune forward is deemed—for whatever reason—a problem.

Maybe this was why Prince was so quiet about his charity. After the Purple One's death, news broke that he had a history of secret altruism (Grow 2016). You might be asking why "The Artist" would hide his giving under a bushel if "God loves a cheerful giver" (2 Corinthians 9:7). Maybe Prince knew better.

In the court of public opinion, not all people so easily fit into God's Plan. Some may read that last sentence as a damning statement, but it could just as easily be read as liberating. Were people to scrutinize the character of our benefactors it probably wouldn't take long for us

62   *Fabricating Authenticity*

to find characteristics with which we wouldn't want to identify. Grace then becomes a tool that saves us from having to return the investment or make reparations. All of a sudden, the virtue of giving isn't so black and white. *Ain't that the gospel truth?*

Richard Newton is Associate Professor of Religious Studies at the University of Alabama. He is author of *Identifying Roots: Alex Haley and the Anthropology of Scriptures* (Equinox Publishing Ltd., 2020) and former editor of the *Bulletin for the Study of Religion*. Newton is also curator of the social media professional development network, *Sowing the Seed: Fruitful Conversations in Religion, Culture and Teaching* (SowingTheSeed.org).

References

Blink-182 (2001). "The Rock Show." Directed by The Malloys. May 2001. Music video, 03:07. Posted 17 June 2009. Retrieved from https://www.youtube.com/watch?v=z7hhDINyBP0.

Bourdieu, Pierre (1986). "The Forms of Culture." In J. G. Richardson (ed.), *Handbook of Theory and Research for the Sociology of Education*, 241–258. New York: Greenwood Press.

Cornelius, Earle (2018). "Rapper Drake's $1M giveaway: Academics Debate Ethics of Publicly Giving Away Money." *LancasterOnline/LNP*. Retrieved from https://lancasteronline.com/features/faith_values/rapper-drake-s-m-giveaway-academics-debate-ethics-of-publicly/article_356410b8-1e40-11e8-81ca-cb596386c64c.html.

Drake (2018). "God's Plan." Directed by Karena Evans. YouTube video, 05:56. Posted 17 February 2018. Retrieved from https://www.youtube.com/watch?v=xpVfcZ0ZcFM.

Grow, Kory (2016). "'Prince, the Secret Philanthropist' His Cause was Humanity.'" *Rolling Stone*, 25 April. Retrieved from https://www.rollingstone.com/culture/culture-news/prince-the-secret-philanthropist-his-cause-was-humanity-157700/.

Jay-Z and Kanye West (2011). "Murder to Excellence." Track 10 on *Watch the Throne*. Roc-A-Fella Records, Roc Nation, and Def Jam Records.

Puckett, Lily (2018). "Remember when Blink-182 made their own "God's Plan" video?" *The Fader*, 16 February. Retrieved from https://www.thefader.com/2018/02/16/remember-when-blink-182-made-their-own-gods-plan-video.

10. Just in It for a Paycheck?: On Philanthrocapitalism, Petro-States, and Paid Protestors

Stacie Swain

Drake's "God's Plan" music video (2018), in which the musician gives out nearly a million dollars, elicits excellent questions about authenticity when it comes to money and acts of giving. For example, does giving money in order to generate attention—and thus, more money—delegitimize the giver's act? In other words, because Drake's philanthropy led to, rather than cut into, a paycheck, was he being inauthentic? Regardless, the fact remains that the video's production and reception take place in the context of the entertainment *industry*—an industry in which artists, producers, critics, distributors, and the like, often make a more-than-comfortable living. In contrast, we should not overlook why those on the receiving end of Drake's philanthropy are so happy to receive the money, as Richard Newton points out (Chapter 9). I want to push this line of questioning further. If we look beyond Drake and his (in)authenticity, what makes the "God's Plan" video a spectacle in the first place?

Without people "in need," Drake (and his critics) couldn't capitalize on his act of giving. In other words, the philanthropic act is conspicuous not only because it was filmed, marketed, and distributed, but more fundamentally because it took place within the context of capitalism: an economic system that seeks to *make* money and *maximize* profit—even through the act of giving money away. To describe this, news sources (The Economist 2006) and scholars coined the term *philanthrocapitalism*: "the idea that *capitalism is or can be charitable in and of itself*," or a situation in which markets and morality provide answers where politics have failed (Thorup 2013: 556, 570–571).

64   *Fabricating Authenticity*

This concept suggests that capitalism and the free market are not the *cause* of social problems but rather, that the market's self-correcting mechanisms will remedy society's ills. Within philanthrocapitalism, those "in need" are left to rely on the beneficence of rich, professionalized individuals—including celebrities like Drake—rather than the state, social programs, or mutual aid. Examining Drake's video via the logic of "celebrity philanthropy," we can see how this form of giving also becomes a way to mark, justify, and legitimize celebrity status (ibid.: 569). Celebrity philanthropy can also include an aspect of emotional affect, in that "one has to feel, engage, participate" and be personally involved with those receiving one's charity (ibid.: 567–568), like Drake when he shares music, hugs, and meaningful moments throughout "God's Plan." Despite Drake's attribution of his success to God, the video leverages the affects of Black joy and gratitude to generate media attention, social capital, and financial profit.

In sum, philanthrocapitalism (re)produces the status quo: a stratified society in which some people are wealthy, while others can't satisfy their needs and wants unless given to. Notably, the recipients of Drake's money primarily appear to be Black families, people of color, and institutions that serve them. As Ruth Wilson Gilmore puts it: "What is the status quo? Put simply, capitalism requires inequality and racism enshrines it" (2015). As Newton implies (Chapter 9), critiques of Drake's authenticity may be racially motivated because his success challenges a white supremacist status quo. Drake's philanthropic act, however, plays within the rules of (philanthro)capitalism. There are two underlying realities worth noting here: (1) the logic of philanthropy does not disrupt the process of accumulation, which means that the profits that rich philanthropists accrue far outstrip what they give away; and (2) conspicuous giving can divert attention away from the ways that those doing the giving have caused or perpetuate inequality in the first place (Cassidy 2015; Hay and Muller 2014; Rhodes and Bloom 2018). The material conditions of capitalism, alongside race and inequality, suggest another context in which authenticity and affect also play a role: the relationship between the petro-state and the paid protestor.

The concept of the *petro-state* describes the codependent relationship between the state and fossil fuel industries, with the hyphen signaling close material and structural ties. Fossil fuel corporations, including those within the petroleum industry, are key players within and across nation-states because our society currently depends upon the resources that these corporations generate their profits from. Not only corporations themselves, but a range of institutions are invested in fossil capital and the petroleum industry (for more see Malm 2016). Public and private institutions bank on these industries—literally banks themselves, but also colleges and universities, pension funds, and religious institutions. Governments like my own, in Canada, provide tax cuts and bailouts to fossil fuel corporations in return for continued business and royalties, while corporate-funded oil and gas lobbyists wield political influence. In the Canadian context, *symbolic nationalization* identifies "a rhetorical strategy through which 'the people' and the petro-industrial complex are sutured together… as if this industry has been nationalized and run to serve the interests of *all* Canadians" (Gunster 2019). Once "wrapped in the flag" so to speak, politicians, corporations, and lobbyists can capitalize on patriotic affect to generate support for the industry or gain votes. On the flip side, politicians, corporations, lobbyists, and mainstream media use the rhetoric of the paid protestor to cast doubt upon the motives of people who challenge the petro-state, extractive industries, and related investments.

Rather than having "authentic" motivations, paid protestor rhetorics declare that those who challenge the petro-state are "frauds" or "fakes" who are just in it a for a paycheck. As such, their motives are enfolded within the capitalist system, as both individualized and self-serving. Further, wrapping extractive industries in the flag, i.e., equating them with national identity, can be used to create the sense that these industries and thus by extension the nation-state itself are under attack by "eco-celebrities" who are "wealthy, hypocritical elites," or "paid protestors" who are "doing the bidding of wealthy U.S. foundations" (Gunster 2019). In this light, those involved are not just *inauthentic* Canadians, they are fundamentally *anti-Canadian*, or may even be "foreign-funded radicals" or "outside agitators" with a covert interest in destabilizing Canada's economy (ibid.). The rhetorical logic of paid protestors, however, relies upon problematic assumptions. As Vicky Osterweil argues:

66   *Fabricating Authenticity*

> This logic strips those who protest of their power, claiming that their experiences, lives, and desires are not actually sufficient to inspire their acts of resistance—implying that they don't know what they're doing. It begins from the presumption that the world is fine as it is, and only nihilistic or paid troublemakers could challenge it. (2020: 6)

As such, the rhetoric of the paid protestor centers the state as the only legitimate source of law and order, with capitalism naturalized as the sole (and ideal) economic system. The petro-state's paid protestor rhetoric, by extension, works to delegitimize political relations that do *not* center the state or conform to capitalist relations.

Nevertheless, those who do not think that "the world is fine as it is" do have (dare I use the term) *authentic* motivations. Such becomes evident when we examine the material realities that underlie resistance to the extractive industries that fuel climate change, environmental degradation, and social disparities. As a report by the UN special rapporteur on extreme poverty and human rights describes, the world is facing a situation of "climate apartheid" in which "the wealthy pay to escape overheating, hunger, and conflict while the rest of the world is left to suffer" (Alston 2019: 12). While corporations and investors profit, racialized, Indigenous, and otherwise marginalized communities disproportionately bear the costs. This dynamic can be understood through the concept of *wastelanding*, which highlights how capitalist economies use discourses of race, class, gender, and/or sexual difference to render some people and places expendable, while others are deemed pristine and deserving of protection (Voyles 2015). The material effects of wastelanding can include poisoned water, earth, or animals, but also manifest as places that are ravaged by rising sea levels, wildfires, and extreme weather events. Wastelanding affects people by way of their environment, but also produces social infrastructure-deprived areas that lack access to clean water, sanitation, health services, education facilities, and/or food security.

In sum, capitalist economies rely upon systems of domination and exploitation that require inequality, profiting some at the expense of others. Another system, closely linked and relevant to the Canadian and U.S. contexts, is *settler colonialism*. Drawing on Cedric Robinson's account of racial capitalism as a system "in which a single white man owns more wealth and land than entire Indigenous nations," Nick Estes explains the relationship between these processes and structures:

> Capitalism arose under a racist feudal system. It used "race" as a form of rule—to subordinate, to kill, and to enslave others—and used that difference for profit-making. Racial capitalism was exported globally as imperialism, including to North America in the form of settler colonialism. As a result, the colonized and racialized poor are still burdened with the most harmful effects of capitalism and climate change, and this is why they are at the forefront of resistance (2019: 28).

Within settler colonial contexts such as the U.S. and Canada, citizens of diverse Indigenous nations not only disproportionately bear the costs of capitalism, but often comprise the forefront of anti-colonial, anti-capitalist, and environmental resistance. As Glen Coulthard puts it, "For Indigenous nations to live, capitalism must die," by which he means that the settler colonial-capitalist system of commodification, accumulation, and exchange is incommensurable with how Indigenous nations relate to the lands, waters, and other-than-human beings (Coulthard 2013). Further, Indigenous *nations* are harmed when their territories are harmed, because they draw their laws, governance systems, and socio-economic orders from those relations. Indigenous resistance, therefore, should not be understood as civil disobedience to Canadian laws (see Borrows 2016). Rather, citizens of Indigenous nations may be obeying *their own laws* to protect place and people from exploitation. Within Indigenous frameworks of law and order, those who challenge capitalism and settler colonialism may be understood as *water protectors or land defenders*. These terms reject the categorization of *protestor*—paid or not—to center roles and responsibilities drawn from Indigenous political and legal orders.

To conclude, concepts like philanthrocapitalism, petro-states, and paid protesters help to make visible the material realities that underlie authenticity discourses. In the Canadian petro-state, following the money can also lead us back to philanthrocapitalism, with

68 *Fabricating Authenticity*

privately-owned oil companies and billionaires channeling funding to police forces through charitable foundations (Lukacs and Groves 2020). These police forces constitute the coercive arm of the colonial-capitalist state apparatus—they are literally *paid* to quell anti-colonial, anti-capitalist struggles for survival and liberation—when the persuasive technique of the paid protestor rhetoric fails to dispel resistance. Moreover, the policing and the judicial branches of settler colonial states are complicit in the oppression of the very communities that Drake gives money to in the "God's Plan" video, a crucial point to note in light of widespread, Black-led uprisings against police brutality (see Angela Davis 1971; Camp and Heatherton 2016; Maynard 2017). Accounting for the material realities beneath authenticity discourse elicits a critically important question: who's really in it for a paycheck? Those who engage in collective struggle against systems of exploitation and domination—or the constellation of corporate, state, and police apparatuses that uphold an oppressive status quo?

Stacie Swain is a doctoral candidate in the Department of Political Science at the University of Victoria, in Lekwungen territories, where she completed an Indigenous Nationhood Graduate Certificate in 2020. Her research considers Indigenous ceremony within public spaces and institutions, with a primary focus on questions of settler colonialism, political authority, and jurisdiction.

References

Alston, Philip, and UN, Human Rights Council, Special Rapporteur on Extreme Poverty and Human Rights (2019). *Climate change and poverty: Report of the Special Rapporteur on Extreme Poverty and Human Rights*. Geneva, Switzerland: UN (17 July). Retrieved from https://undocs.org/A/HRC/41/39.

Borrows, John (2016). *Freedom and Indigenous Constitutionalism*. Toronto, Buffalo, London: University of Toronto Press.

Camp, Jordan T., and Christina Heatherton (eds.) (2016). *Policing the Planet: Why the Policing Crisis Led to Black Lives Matter*. London; New York: Verso.

Cassidy, John (2015). "Mark Zuckerberg and the Rise of Philanthrocapitalism." *The New Yorker*, 3 December. Retrieved from https://www.newyorker.com/news/john-cassidy/mark-zuckerberg-and-the-rise-of-philanthrocapitalism.

Coulthard, Glen Sean (2013). "For Our Nations to Live, Capitalism Must Die." *Unsettling America*, 5 November. Retrieved from https://unsettlingamerica.wordpress.com/2013/11/05/for-our-nations-to-live-capitalism-must-die/.

Davis, Angela Y. (1971). "Political Prisoners, Prisons, and Black Liberation," *History is a Weapon* (blog). Retrieved from https://www.historyisaweapon.com/defcon1/davispoprprblli.html.

Drake (2018). "God's Plan." Directed by Karena Evans. YouTube video, 05:56. Posted 17 February 2018. Retrieved from https://www.youtube.com/watch?v=xpVfcZ0ZcFM.

Economist, The (2006). "The Birth of Philanthrocapitalism." *The Economist*, 9 (US), 25 February. Retrieved from https://www.economist.com/special-report/2006/02/25/the-birth-of-philanthrocapitalism.

Gilmore, Ruth Wilson (2015). "The Worrying State of the Anti-Prison Movement," *Social Justice* (blog), 23 February. Retrieved from (web archive) http://archive.today/2022.06.23-112750/http://www.socialjusticejournal.org/the-worrying-state-of-the-anti-prison-movement/.

Gunster, Shane (2019). "Extractive Populism and the Future of Canada." *The Monitor*, 2 July. Retrieved from https://www.policyalternatives.ca/publications/monitor/extractive-populism-and-future-canada.

Hay, Iain, and Samantha Muller (2014). "Questioning Generosity in the Golden Age of Philanthropy: Towards Critical Geographies of Super-Philanthropy." *Progress in Human Geography* 38/5: 635–653. https://doi.org/10.1177/0309132513500893

Lukacs, Martin, and Tim Groves (2020). "Private Firms Pour Millions into Militarizing Police via Charities." *The Tyee*, 24 August. Retrieved from https://thetyee.ca/News/2020/08/24/Private-Firms-Pour-Millions-Militarizing-Police/.

Malm, Andreas (2016). *Fossil Capital: The Rise of Steam Power and the Roots of Global Warming*. Brooklyn, NY; London: Verso Books.

Maynard, Robyn (2017). *Policing Black Lives: State Violence in Canada from Slavery to the Present*. Fernwood Publishing.

Osterweil, Vicky (2020). *In Defense of Looting: A Riotous History of Uncivil Action*. New York: Bold Type Books.

Rhodes, Carl, and Peter Bloom (2018). "The Trouble with Charitable Billionaires." *The Guardian*, 24 May. Retrieved from https://www.theguardian.com/news/2018/may/24/the-trouble-with-charitable-billionaires-philanthrocapitalism.

70   *Fabricating Authenticity*

Thorup, Mikkel (2013). "Pro Bono? On Philanthrocapitalism as Ideological Answer to Inequality." *Ephemera* 13/3: 555–576. http://www.ephemerajournal.org/contribution/ pro-bono-philanthrocapitalism-ideological-answer-inequality

Voyles, Traci Brynne (2015). *Wastelanding: Legacies of Uranium Mining in Navajo Country*. Minneapolis: University of Minnesota Press.

11. On the Tyranny of Individualism: MAGA Boy, Media, and the Drum

Matt Sheedy

This piece's first incarnation began as a draft for a blog post on January 19, 2019, one day after a short video featuring a group of high school students taunting a Native American man went viral. When I returned to the piece a few days later, the story had blown-up like few that I can recall in recent memory. The initial narrative, which was clipped from a two-hour video, posted on Twitter (Conger and Frankel 2019), and seized upon by the press, created the perception that the high school students had surrounded Nathan Phillips (Mervosh 2019), an Omaha elder and activist, sparking outrage across the media spectrum. At the center of all this was the image of a young man in a MAGA hat (Make America Great Again, a popular slogan of Donald Trump) staring smugly at Phillips as he played a (Native American) drum-song.

Once the extended two-hour video emerged, this narrative quickly gave way to a feverish debate over the mainstream media's "liberal" bias, and their rush to condemn the boys before getting the full picture of what took place by the Lincoln Memorial in Washington, D.C. Accordingly, much of the press turned the lens on themselves through acts of contrition, as with the following CBC News article, "Rush to judgment on Covington school standoff should be a wake-up call for media" (Urback 2019).

One of the more interesting exchanges on the media's initial response to this story came from the popular podcast, *The Joe Rogan Experience*. In this interview, Rogan sits down with *The New York Times* columnist Bari Weiss to discuss the fallout from this affair,

72 *Fabricating Authenticity*

where Weiss pontificates on what was wrong with the media's initial response.

> The challenge of what it means to be a journalist is to not see people as *signifiers* or as *stand-ins* just based on their identity. And that's what 95% of the press core did... They leap to assume that our visceral reaction was accurate, when in fact, when you actually look at the two-hour video ... it was not that at all.

A little later in the interview, Weiss quips:

> WEISS: My thing is, your initial reaction to something is not the truth. It's your *emotional reaction*. And anyone who calls themselves a journalist, like your job is to figure out the facts of the case, not to make this into a kind of identitarian morality play. And the fact that so many people, in so many publications did just that, and in fact, when the real facts surfaced just sort of dug their heels in and were basically like, "Well he's a stand-in for the white patriarchy." What? That's crazy! ... You're really going to put that on a sixteen-year-old?
>
> JOE ROGAN: Well, it's cruel. It's a denial of the individual. It's very cruel. Um, when you're sixteen years old, you're basically a baby. You don't know what the fuck you're doing ... you're incredibly susceptible to the influence of your peers. (JRE Clips 2019)

While it is true that the boys did not surround Nathan Phillips (he had in fact approached them), and were likely confused by his drumming, which Phillip's claims was an attempt to de-escalate a shouting match between the students and a group of Black Israelites who were involved in a separate protest (Sidner 2019), Weiss and Rogan's emphasis on the specific details of this incident reflect what I am here calling the *tyranny of individualism*. By this I mean the tendency, especially in Euro-Western cultures, to center the individual as the locus of meaning (e.g., their agency, beliefs, and intentions). This often results in downplaying (or ignoring) how "signifiers" provoke "emotional reactions" precisely because they "stand-in" as symbols for the divergent experiences of different social groups and reflect their (unequal) relationship and access to power. In this sense, even if the initial response to this story was distorted, it still "signifies" a broader set of concerns that point beyond this isolated incident. Why else would it provoke such a strong reaction? What is more, the asymmetries of power to create, shape, and control narratives like this one are contingent upon existing fields of knowledge, where certain symbols and language can rely on a degree of intelligibility among the general public, while others cannot. For example, many of us may "know" what a MAGA hat might represent, but how many are able to interpret a "Native American" drum song?

By way of analogy, in her book *This is Why We Can't Have Nice Things*, Whitney Phillips touches on one of the ways that signifiers function with reference to the common use of the "n-word" among online trolls, who will often claim when challenged that it's not meant to be racist, it's just "for the lulz." As she writes:

> [T]rolls are fully aware that this word is the furthest thing from a floating, meaningless signifier. In fact, they depend on the political significance of all the epithets they employ. Echoing Judith Butler's analysis of hate speech, which posits that racial epithets always already gesture toward their own history regardless of what a person means when he or she uses hateful language, trolls need their language to contain a kernel of hate. From the trolls' perspective, this is a purely practical point. If the epithets in question weren't politically contentious, they would be useless as trollbait (2015: 96).

Following (Whitney) Phillips' analysis, I want to suggest that part of what guided the strong and polarized reaction to this story is how it appealed to different sets of signifiers, which are attached to competing group identities.

For those sympathetic to the Covington High School boys, the image of a lone Indigenous elder beating a drum in a crowd of cheering and jeering teenagers did not appear, at first, to offer any sort of defense of their behavior. It just looked bad. When the two-hour video emerged, however, it not only provided the boys with some plausible deniability (e.g., they did not surround Phillips as initially reported), but also created a counter-narrative where they could be

74   *Fabricating Authenticity*

positioned as victims—of a "liberal" media that has increasingly been characterized as "fake news," and of the Black Israelites, who were taunting them in a way that was read as an attack on their whiteness, and on their conservative Christian values. Thus, a victim narrative was born to counter-act the strong indictment that the initial viral image produced.

For those sympathetic to Nathan Philips, the image of a young white man in a MAGA hat staring-down an Indigenous elder signified not only an embodiment of power and privilege (read: white, young, and male, etc.), but also conveyed a feeling of callous disrespect through his particular mode of defiance (i.e., his expression, his hat, and his presence among a large group of jeering friends), signaling that he was the one in control and had nothing to fear. For anyone familiar with the history of race relations in America, including settler-colonialism and its effects on Native Americans, one could hardly imagine a more pointed symbol (and reminder) of past and current power dynamics reflected in a single pose.

Much else could be added to this narrative, depending on what sources one pays attention to, including the two very different reasons that brought the boys and Phillips to the National Mall—the anti-abortion March for Life and the Indigenous Peoples March—adding further layers of religion, gender, sexuality, and race into the mix. The Covington boys even received support from Donald Trump and were offered an official invite to the White House (Riotta 2019), which highlights the role of political power in shaping the symbolic field.

Although all of these narratives are plausible, depending on one's prior sympathies, connection to certain signifiers, etc., if we turn our attention to the "agonistic [or public] moment of these claims," and the "broader socio-political issues driving this particular moment of contest," as Andie Alexander and Jason W. M. Ellsworth write in the introduction to this volume, any "official" or "authentic" representation of events is shown to be a product of an asymmetrical power-play, where the prior ideological commitments of those with a platform (such as those of Weiss and Rogan) carry the greatest weight.

This incident thus offers a poignant example of how dominant groups are able to shape public narratives by virtue of what symbols, ideologies, histories, and forms of knowledge have been naturalized in the mainstream imagination, especially when juxtaposed with those that remain relatively obscure or unknown. This is especially true of Indigenous-centered narratives, which barely registered in most mainstream reporting (Cuthand 2019), despite the centrality of an elder with a drum. As famed Lakota political prisoner Leonard Peltier writes—in his own authenticity narrative—the song that Phillips was singing was a "religious song" gifted to the American Indian Movement by the Northern Cheyenne People, who created it in response to the Wounded Knee Massacre of 1890 (Peltier 2019). In this sense, signifiers that aren't generally understood by the majority (e.g., how many readers "know" what I'm referring to?) tell us something about the relationship between knowledge and power, as well as how marginalized identities are often read through more popular signifiers (e.g., as left-wing protest, or racism/victimization in general, etc.) as their symbols are defined on outsiders' terms.

Addendum

Following the initial draft of this essay, Nicholas Sandmann (aka "MAGA boy") sued CNN for $275 million, along with *The Washington Post* and other outlets, receiving an undisclosed settlement (Fair 2020). On August 25, 2020, Sandmann was a featured speaker at the Republican National Convention's (RNC) official nomination of Donald Trump for president. Sandmann spoke of being a victim of the news media, the Left, and of professional protesters who wanted to "cancel" him. He also affirmed his support for Trump, who he characterized as a defender of objective journalism and free speech (PBS NewsHour 2020). I had initially left Nicholas Sandmann's name out of this piece precisely because of the negative attention he was getting as a sixteen-year-old who, as an individual, did not ask for such publicity. In July of 2020, Sandmann turned eighteen, and elected to speak at the RNC, which changes the calculus considerably.

Whatever else might be said about the role of social media in producing hasty reporting and negative consequences (e.g., so-called "cancel-culture"), adding fuel to the already volatile culture wars, it

76 *Fabricating Authenticity*

is clear that Sandmann was able to utilize this incident to considerable advantage. In the interim since January 2019, Sandmann has benefited financially (substantially, by the sound of it!), and has not been the target of further harassment—or, at least, has not spoken of such things as an ongoing concern. In this sense, his agency was affirmed through the legal system in ways that could be interpreted to reflect certain privileges that his status as a young, white, conservative, Christian-identifying male enabled. By contrast, I am not aware of any similar financial settlements made by media outlets to Black or Indigenous persons for an initially one-sided news story that resulted in online harassment. Beyond the clear affirmation of Sandmann's agency *as an individual*, we might also ask what subsequent developments following this incident signify on a broader social level?

In the asymmetrical power-play that I refer to above, issues of identity politics, media bias, and ideological framing—what I refer to as the tyranny of individualism—resulted in a victim narrative and subsequently, an outcome that favored Nicholas Sandmann and seemingly vindicated all of the "signifiers" attached to his name. His speech at the RNC not only confirms the initial narrative (at least for those sympathetic to his claims), but also expands his story of victimhood into newer chains of signification. This includes allusions to "free speech" and "cancel culture," while positioning Donald Trump as an antidote to "fake news," "the Left," and "professional protesters." In the context of 2020, these latter two terms have become attached to the unrest following the police murder of George Floyd on May 25, and thus merge with additional narratives blaming Antifa and the Black Lives Matter movement as the main cause of chaos in the streets throughout the United States. Lastly, the scant attention to Nathan Phillips' in the initial story appears to have followed in lockstep with the pattern that I lay out above. Here his Indigenous identity, along with the many issues that that entails, has been erased, replaced by popular signifiers such as "the Left" and "protesters," which functions, to quote Bari Weiss, as its own "identitarian morality play," though not the one she had mind.

Matt Sheedy holds a Ph.D. in the study of religion and is a visiting professor in North American Studies at the University of Bonn, Germany. His research interests include critical social theory, theories of religion and secularism, as well as discourses on Islam, atheism, new age, and Native American traditions in popular and political culture. He is the author of *Owning the Secular: Religious Symbols, Culture Wars, Western Fragility* (Routledge, 2021). His current book project is entitled, Islam According to Google News: How Media Shape the Way We Talk About Religion.

References

Conger, Kate, and Sheera Frenkel (2019). "Who Posted Viral Video of Covington Students and Protester? Congress Wants to Know." *The New York Times*, 23 January. Retrieved from https://www.nytimes.com/2019/01/23/technology/covington-video-protester-congress.html (accessed 15 December 2019).

Cuthand, Doug (2019). "Importance of Indigenous Peoples March Got Overshadowed By 'the Face of White Privilege.'" *CBC News*, 26 January. Retrieved from https://www.cbc.ca/news/indigenous/opinion-covington-indigenous-peoples-march-1.4993851 (accessed 15 December 2019).

Fair, Julia (2020). "Nick Sandmann's Settlement with CNN was Almost Public. A Birthday and a Pandemic Changed That." *Cincinnati Enquirer*, 24 August. Retrieved from https://www.cincinnati.com/story/news/2020/08/24/kentucky-nick-sandmann-how-much-settlement-amount-cnn-public-covid-19-delay/3428644001/ (accessed 26 August 2020).

JRE Clips (2019). "Joe Rogan on the 'MAGA' Kids Controversy." YouTube video, 19:38. Posted 21 January 2019. Retrieved from https://www.youtube.com/watch?v=MjV7EDuL21M&t=812s (accessed 15 December 2019).

Mervosh, Sarah (2019). "Viral Video Shows Boys in 'Make America Great Again' Hats Surrounding Native Elder." *The New York Times*, 20 January. Retrieved from https://www.nytimes.com/2019/01/19/us/covington-catholic-high-school-nathan-phillips.html?searchResultPosition=1 (accessed 15 December 2019).

PBS NewsHour (2020). "Nicholas Sandmann's Full Speech at the Republican National Convention, 2020." YouTube video, 04:34. Posted 25 August 2020. https://www.youtube.com/watch?v=tCDsBS2Ljqk (accessed 26 August 2020).

78 *Fabricating Authenticity*

Peltier, Leonard (2019). "Leonard Peltier: How Native Elder Nathan Phillips Defeated the MAGA Punks with a Song." *The San Francisco Bay View National Black Newspaper*, 22 January. Retrieved from https://sfbayview.com/2019/01/leonard-peltier-how-native-elder-nathan-phillips-defeated-the-maga-punks-with-a-song/ (accessed 15 December 2019).

Philips, Whitney (2015). *This is Why We Can't Have Nice Things. Mapping the Relationship Between On-Line Trolling and Mainstream Culture.* Cambridge, MA: MIT Press.

Riotta, Chris (2019). "White House Invites Covington Catholic Students as Nick Sandmann Speaks Out on National TV." *The Independent*, 23 January. Retrieved from https://www.independent.co.uk/news/world/americas/us-politics/covington-catholic-high-school-video-trump-white-house-invite-nick-sandmann-a8742671.html (accessed 15 December 2019).

Sidner, Sara (2019). "Native American Elder Nathan Phillips, in His Own Words." *CNN*, 12 March. Retrieved from https://edition.cnn.com/2019/01/21/us/nathan-phillips-maga-teens-interview/index.html (accessed 15 December 2019).

Urback, Robyn (2019). "Rush to Judgement on Covington School Standoff Should Be a Wake-up Call for Media." *CBC News*, 21 January. Retrieved from https://www.cbc.ca/news/opinion/covington-stand-off-1.4987065 (accessed 15 December 2019).

12. Symbols and Ownership

Yasmine Flodin-Ali

Matt Sheedy's chapter posits that the individual is seen as the ultimate signifier of meaning in many so-called Western societies. In the United States, the archetype of the individual is depicted as a fully self-reliant, clearly bounded, autonomous entity. These characteristics can take on almost mythic proportions, which Sheedy describes as "the tyranny of individualism." For example, for many the American dream venerates the idea of hard-working individuals who "pull themselves up by their bootstraps," and carve out better lives for themselves without any outside help. This remains a dream because it is highly aspirational: Can anyone truly claim to exist outside of social bonds, without being beholden to anyone?

I contend that for those who have the privilege of demarcating themselves as individuals do so at the expense of those who are always represented as part of a collective. News outlets repeatedly emphasized that "the MAGA boy," Nicholas Sandmann, was sixteen years old. Yet young men of color are frequently portrayed by the media as adults. In the scenario Sheedy examines, Nicholas is interviewed and engaged as an individual, whereas no one person is selected from the Black Israelite group to be interviewed. The Black Israelite group continues to be depicted as a mass.

While this is a single case, I argue that actions of individual people of color are typically painted as representative of their designated identity groups, especially when those actions are seen as negative. Yet white men who commit violence are often described as mentally ill and lone wolves, rendering their motivations as highly personal and disconnected from larger demographic patterns. One famous *Family Guy* meme illustrates this phenomenon well: the main character Peter holds a color swatch that goes from white to brown to black,

80   *Fabricating Authenticity*

a sliding scale that corresponds with the labels "Mentally ill" and "Terrorist" respectively. Questions of who gets to claim individuality are essentially questions of which people society deems fully human. Whiteness is the category that society deems as the default.

Sheedy notes that "signifiers" provoke "emotional reactions" because they speak to the well-being and state of larger groups of people. This is not unique to so-called Western societies. I say "so-called Western societies" because binary notions of the West and East, which imply self-evidently distinct locations while ignoring their intertwined histories and the layers of diversity within identity groups. The complexities of the world are not so easily divided into two categories. The power and impact of group symbols is not negated by the prevalence of "American individualism." As Sheedy points out, a MAGA hat immediately conjures up a specific set of associations. Similarly, people who proudly fly the confederate flag in the name of heritage are referencing particular political positions and a specific set of historical events that led to the formation of that symbol (SPLC 2019).

Different sets of signifiers appeal to the different social groupings with which people identify. A larger American audience may not be familiar with the nuanced signifiers of a Native American drum song as in the case examined by Sheedy previously, so it is important to remember how power dynamics can also structure how the same symbol is interpreted differently depending on the group's perspective. The symbology of minority groups is frequently appropriated by the majority. As Andie Alexander and Jason W. M. Ellsworth explain in their introduction to this volume, the "official or authentic" representation of events is frequently a result of asymmetrical power systems.

For example, an Islamic prayer rug might signify a range of things to a Muslim audience, including ritual, piety, comfort, or even guilt, depending on the person. In 2019, when President Trump made the baseless claim that prayer rugs had been found at the U.S.-Mexico border, he invoked rugs as a symbol of otherness (Qiu 2019). In a fascinating rhetorical turn, Trump collapsed two different racialized threats of "brown people"—that is, stereotypes about Mexican immigrants and stereotypes about Muslim South Asian and Arab immigrants—into one larger threat. (There are Latinx Muslims, but Trump's particular use of symbology does not seem to be pointing towards such a nuanced analysis). The primary purpose of Trump using the imagery of a prayer rug is to speak to a white Christian base that sees themselves as under siege. The prayer rug becomes almost anthropomorphized, a stand-in for the brown bodies ready to infiltrate a rightfully white, Protestant America.

Differences in interpretation of symbols are largely dependent on power relations, and, relatedly, on networks of information. Social media has increasingly siloed us from one another. We consume knowledge from different sources, which leads us to different perceptions of reality. To an extent this has always been the case—different communities have different stakes in current events which affect how they relate to information; but it's difficult to deny the acceleration of this fracturing in our current media age. The online group QAnon is famous for its elaborate symbology, stitching together seemingly unrelated events to form grand meta-narratives, which is why they are often labeled as conspiracy theorists (Wong 2020). People who ascribe to this series of conspiracy theories are able to exist in echo-chamber mediascapes that help form and then reify their worldviews.

The last aspect that Sheedy's piece leads us to examine is the question of who is deemed worthy of being a victim. In the initial clip shown of the incident Sheedy discusses, the white Covington High School boys appeared to be mocking a Native American man. A longer segment of footage later revealed a more complicated story, pointing to the fact that both right and left mediascapes can become bubbles with their own echo chambers. For many, the Covington boys were seen as victims of an intentional smear campaign. As Sheedy relates in his conclusion, one member of the group, Nicholas Sandmann, went on to speak at the Republican National Convention in 2020. Narratives of victimization do not always match the material realities of their proponents. From the standpoint of those with power, the creation of more equitable playing fields can feel like a loss of power, and the use of victimization narratives works to authorize the group's socio-political agenda.

82 *Fabricating Authenticity*

Yasmine Flodin-Ali is Assistant Professor of Modern Islam and Race at the University of Pittsburgh's Department of Religious Studies. Her current book project maps the landscape of early twentieth century Muslim movements in the United States.

References

Qiu, Linda (2019). "Trump's Baseless Claim About Prayer Rugs Found at the Border." *The New York Times*, 18 January. Retrieved from https://www.nytimes.com/2019/01/18/us/politics/fact-check-trump-prayer-rugs-border.html.

SPLC (2019). "Whose Heritage? Public Symbols of the Confederacy." *Southern Poverty Law Center*, 1 February. Retrieved from https://www.splcenter.org/20190201/whose-heritage-public-symbols-confederacy.

Wong, Julia Carrie (2020). "QAnon Explained: The Antisemitic Conspiracy Theory Gaining Traction Around the World." *The Guardian*, 25 August. Retrieved from https://www.theguardian.com/us-news/2020/aug/25/qanon-conspiracy-theory-explained-trump-what-is.

13. Donald Trump: A "Baby Christian"?

Leslie Dorrough Smith

Back in the summer of 2016, James Dobson, noted evangelical leader and founder of the Focus on the Family empire, made the public claim that then-presidential candidate Donald Trump had become a born-again Christian (Gabriel and Luo 2016). This statement was made largely in an attempt to explain how Trump's string of unsavory comments and crude vocabulary need not repel the "values voters" who Dobson represented and whose support Trump so desperately needed to win the election. When asked to reconcile his claim with Trump's language, Dobson located the reason for Trump's behaviors in the fact that he was a "baby Christian," or very recent convert. In other words, Dobson argued, Trump should be given a pass in the matter of his foul language and otherwise distasteful comments since he was not raised in an evangelical environment and was just learning the cultural ropes, so to speak (ibid.).

By October of that same year, the infamous Billy Bush interview with Trump would electrify the political scene. The video featured Trump more than a decade earlier talking openly with Bush about how he grabbed and groped beautiful women because he could. Although Trump initially denied that the tape was real, he later dismissed it as simply "locker room talk." Once again, prominent evangelicals supported Trump, including Dobson, but instead of reinforcing the "baby Christian" idea again, many simply described him as the political vehicle for their social policy (Gray 2016). Despite the fact that statements specifically discussing Trump's own religiosity may ebb and flow, there has been no end to the evangelical spokespersons who continue to identify him as a specifically religious instrument.

84 *Fabricating Authenticity*

In what we now know is a very predicable ping-pong effect, a wave of anti-Trump folks has responded to the "baby Christian" and other religiously positive appellations regarding Trump with the claim that his ethics have been so bankrupt that this news couldn't possibly be taken seriously. Yet as Russell McCutcheon has argued in response, the progressive clamor over whether Trump's religiosity is "genuine" is actually a conservative move in the sense that it presumes the existence of some sort of authentic religious experience that is deemed authoritative and positive precisely because it is presumed apolitical (McCutcheon 2016). McCutcheon's analysis points to the fact that since every religious act is designed to have some impact on the power relationships shared by people (that is, society), every such act is political in one way or another. So while Trump may be among the more colorful candidates to invoke religion while on the campaign trail and during his time in office, there's nothing particularly unique in how he's doing it.

Instead of asking about the authenticity of a politician's religious utterances, the far more interesting—and verifiable—function of their discourse offers us much more in terms of cultural analysis. In other words, might we ask how the concept of a "baby Christian" or similar notions works as a rhetorical device in this particular cultural setting? What would be at stake if, instead of discussing how Trump does or does not measure up to certain ethical or theological standards, we instead focused on what ends are achieved through such a labeling system?

In saying this, I'm reminded of Naomi Klein's now classic work, *No Logo*, in which, among other things, Klein argues that what we buy when we purchase the products of multi-billion-dollar corporations are not the products themselves as much as the brand that those products represent. Branding is, in this sense, not just advertising, but the multitude of efforts to interact with the public that generates certain feelings about the company and its place in society (Klein 2019). It doesn't matter whether my new Nikes actually make me run faster or with greater comfort; I am likely compelled to buy them because Nike's branding efforts help me associate strength, exercise, grit, and victory with myself once those shoes go on my feet. Klein's point, simply put, is that capitalism depends just as much on the exchange of certain types of emotions rather than in the more tangible goods and services we often associate with the term.

I am thus interested in thinking through the "baby Christian" label not as a theological statement, nor as a neutral descriptor, but as a logo that has more easily facilitated the persuasive work that Trump has needed to perform. I call this characterization of Trump a logo because its social function is quite simple: its job has been to sell his brand by synthesizing a series of symbols that cast him as a member of a desirable group ("Christian"). The modifier "baby" was required to mitigate the fact that, on many levels, he failed to meet the broad stereotypes often associated with that group, and yet it also allowed him to retain full membership.

But we should not take the need for the modifier "baby" too seriously here, for, after all, there are millions of racist, sexist, cussing melagomaniacs who identify as Christians. In other words, Trump was and is not a rare breed. Dobson's words were thus not about the necessity of a certain type of moral code to be called a Christian, however much they may appear to be; instead, Dobson was and is a large cog in a branding campaign the success of which is not measured in gauging things called "penitence" or "spiritual insights," but in winning votes by persuading millions of otherwise very diverse people to get behind a vaguely positive symbol.

There is, of course, an irony here, for despite the hundreds of hours that were lost as commentators hashed through the details of Trump's theological insights, those of us who study the work of powerful cultural symbols know that they must remain vague to be effective. How else can one person appeal to an audience of millions unless they are symbolically allied to generalized positive feelings that can be transformed into whatever the viewer or listener wishes to see or hear? Almost by definition, then, claims that Trump was a Christian could not have meant anything specific if they were to be effective in the political sphere. Trump's Christianity serves the same function as the Nike Swoosh or the Target Bullseye: its job is to convey a series of vague feelings and little more.

86   *Fabricating Authenticity*

Leslie Dorrough Smith is Professor of Religious Studies at Avila University (Kansas City, MO), where she is also the Director of the Women's and Gender Studies Program. She is co-author (with Steven W. Ramey) of *Religions of the World: Questions, Challenges, and New Directions* (Equinox Publishing Ltd., 2024) and author of *Compromising Positions: Sex Scandals, Politics, and American Christianity* (Oxford, 2020) and *Righteous Rhetoric: Sex, Speech, and the Politics of Concerned Women for America* (Oxford, 2014). Her research interests focus on American conservative Protestants, critical theory, and the use of method and theory in both religious studies and gender studies.

References

Gabriel, Trip, and Michael Luo (2016). "A Born-Again Donald Trump? Believe It, Evangelical Leader Says." *The New York Times*, 25 June. Retrieved from https://www.nytimes.com/2016/06/26/us/politics/a-born-again-donald-trump-believe-it-evangelical-leader-says.html.

Gray, Rosie (2016). "Prominent Evangelicals Still Backing Trump After Lewd Video." *BuzzFeed News*, 8 October. Retrieved from https://www.buzzfeednews.com/article/rosiegray/prominent-evangelicals-still-backing-trump-after-graphic-vid.

Klein, Naomi (2019). *No Logo*. London: Picador.

McCutcheon, Russell T. (2016). "Make A Shift," *Studying Religion in Culture* (blog), 27 June. Retrieved from https://religion.ua.edu/blog/2016/06/27/make-a-shift/.

14. An Orbiter Is a Simp, a Foid Is a Foid

Nevada S. Drollinger-Smith

In 1997, a Toronto resident created Alanna's Involuntary Celibacy Project. Alanna sought to create a space where adults who had trouble forming long-term relationships or finding romantic partners could meet and discuss loneliness and their shared challenges. In the intervening years, involuntary celibate (incel) communities have changed significantly, although the aim of creating community remains the same. These communities were thrust into the spotlight in 2014 when Elliot Rodger killed six people and injured fourteen others in Isla Vista, California; his rage was inspired primarily by his lack of success with women. And then, in April 2018, Alek Minassian drove a rented van into pedestrians for several blocks in Toronto, Ontario. Minassian allegedly made a Facebook post before the attack, which read, "Private (Recruit) Minassian Infantry 00010, wishing to speak to Sgt 4chan please. C23249161. The Incel Rebellion has already begun! We will overthrow all the Chads and Stacys! All hail the Supreme Gentleman Elliot Rodger!" (Madhani and Bacon 2018). Minassian's attack, and his explicit connections to inceldom, prompted a rash of newspaper and magazine articles wondering where this community had originated.

Incels are often described as violent misogynists, and that is the extent of what many people know about the community. A perusal of Incels.co, one of the fora devoted to discussion of inceldom, demonstrates this well. However, incel discourse is also often rife with talk of just what makes an incel an incel. For many in the community, the ultimate incel must be a kissless, touchless, hugless, handholdless virgin (KTHHV), and there are myriad of reasons as to why this

88 *Fabricating Authenticity*

might be the case. Incels heavily cite evolutionary biology and race science to support their conclusions about both their romantic prospects and their obligation to adhere to social norms. For example, one poster on the now-defunct Incels.me forum writes,

> Women and society have dejected us into loneliness and depression. Their obsession with looks has driven many of us who don't fit their standards to anger and homicidal tendencies. This is not the result of mental illness, it is a normal response to prejudiced behavior...What's the incentive for incels (ugly men) to follow YOUR social rules, when our actions, good or bad, will never be rewarded? ... Why NOT shoot up that sorority full of girls that teased you? (quoted in Cook 2018)

Another aspect considered essential to true inceldom is the notion of the Red Pill/Black Pill. To be Red Pilled means that an incel recognizes the so-called truth that female degeneracy, hypergamy, and feminism have all created the social circumstances that cause men to be rejected for their appearance or mental health. To be Black Pilled is to further recognize that it is impossible to subvert these circumstances, and so a "true incel" will always be an incel. By and large the "true incel" is the inverse of the "real" man: for incels don't have sex, financial stability, robust mental health, physical strength, or good bone structure. True incels must also always be men, because sexual dissatisfaction and loneliness are a uniquely male circumstance (Alptraum 2018). By contrast, an orbiter will "simp" for women, orbiting around them and attending to their needs and wishes in the hopes of gaining sexual or romantic attention. Even if an orbiter is celibate, this kind of behavior is not considered appropriate for a true incel. Of course, these specific criteria can be contested. For instance, an incel who has sex with a sex worker may still be considered an incel. However, I contend that meeting the specific criteria to be an incel matters less than cultivating a specific orientation to a truth about men, women, relationships, and success. In other words, it ultimately doesn't matter much whether an incel is "really" a KTHHV. How would anyone be able to tell in any case?

The sense of being losers who are unlucky at love permeates these men's descriptions of themselves and their interactions with one another. However, this is not necessarily the point. What we can take from the discourse of the Red and Black Pills is that what is at stake here is not engaging in a sexual relationship, but instead is the cultivation of a relationship to "truth" or "reality" of femininity, masculinity, and privilege. Much as Leslie Dorrough Smith argues, the label of incel is less about a specific mode of being in the world, and more about how the label functions for these men.

These self-described losers could not have asked for a better public relations champion than Naama Kates, whose podcast, *Incel,* features interviews with members from Incels.co. The podcast offers a platform for incels to tell their personal stories with minimal intervention or pushback from Kates. Her goal is to bring greater understanding to the incel community, and, it seems, to mitigate their culpability for or complicity in the violent actions of self-proclaimed members. For instance, in the eighth episode of *Incel,* Kates argues that, in spite of his own claims, Minassian was not radicalized by incel communities online, and that even if he were, it would not matter because he would have become violent in any case (Kates 2019).

In an August 3, 2020 post on the *Incel Blog,* Kates argued that incels are united more by their loneliness than their misogyny and that this is how they ought to be characterized. Alongside this, she contends that incels' respect for intellectual rigor is what they offer society and that, if incels and their ideas seem to be antiquated,

> [Society has] evolved, in large thanks to the antiquated systems of the past, and to the tireless curiosity and dedication of those thinkers who sat off on the sidelines and observed their fellow humans as they danced their strange, ritualistic dance. They bucked at the social consequences of turning inward and asking why, and for that, we owe them a debt of gratitude. (Kates 2020)

Further, she also argues that the derogatory terms that incels use to describe women, such as "hole," "femoid," or "foid," signal that, in fact, they have great respect and longing for "real" women and only denigrate what they imagine women to be. Kates' work, which seeks to explain or humanize incels, also strikes at the heart of how these men understand the nature of the difference between men and women

90   *Fabricating Authenticity*

and how they came to be in the predicament of loneliness to begin with.

When describing the writings of Freikorpsmen, German irregulars but in this case, right-wing paramilitary militiamen in post-WWI Germany, sociologist Klaus Theweleit argues that "a woman to hate" must be created, because people are not simply clusters of attributes assigned to a given category (1987 [1977]: 67). That the woman imagined is fictive does not diminish the sense of satisfaction engendered for many of these men when they see or imagine women killed, mutilated, or sexually assaulted. In contrast to the notion that signifiers are intended to intimate vague feelings, Theweleit argues,

> All of the objects and configurations of which the language of these men incessantly speaks have a definite air of fictionality about them. Historical events are experienced and reported as if in a delirium, but it is a highly controlled, selective delirium. Their feelings, their touch, their language descend on a relatively small number of densely signifying objects and configurations, each of which is invaded by, enveloped in fantasy... as if penned by one single, fictive author. (ibid.: 88)

Ultimately, it doesn't much matter whether or not Foids are representative of "real" women because that's not the point here. Much like the idea of KTHHV, the conception of Foids generates a target and justifies a particular orientation to the "truths" of inceldom.

As Incels.co user nazianime responded to the rumors of Kates' presence on the forums, "Don't incels recognize women as an inferior sub species [*sic*] that human males need to dominate? What is the point of joining an incel/blackpilled forum if you refuse to accept this?" (nazianime 2020). The truths of inceldom continually hinge on the notion that these men's lack of success and prestige is a *fact* of how the world operates and that their helplessness and inability to change the "truth" justifies their rage. The varying discourses of inceldom here help to illustrate the ways in which "truth" and "authenticity" are constructed and used to make sense of one's place in society.

Nevada S. Drollinger-Smith holds an M.A. in Religious Studies and works in Behavioral Health Quality and Compliance.

References

Alpatraum, Lux (2018). "'Unfuckable' Women Don't Go on Killing Sprees," *Splinter News*, 3 May. Retrieved from https://splinternews.com/unfuckable-women-dont-go-on-killing-sprees-1825746733.

Cook, Jessalyn (2018). "Inside Incels' Looksmaxing Obsession: Penis Stretching, Skull Implants, and Rage." *The Huffington Post*, 24 July. Retrieved from https://www.huffingtonpost.co.uk/entry/incels-looksmaxing-obsession_n_5b50e56ee4b0de86f48b0a4f.

Kates, Naama (2019). "The True Believer: The Case of Alek Minassian," Produced by Crawlspace Media. *Incel*. 1 October. Podcast, 35:05. https://anchor.fm/incel/episodes/8-the-true-believer-the-case-of alek-minassian-e5n5fj

———. (2020). "The Misogynistic Spectrum," *Incel Blog*. Retrieved from https://incel.blog/the-misogynistic-spectrum.

Madhani, Aamer, and John Bacon (2018). "Toronto van attack suspect Alek Minassian's Facebook account praised mass killer." *USA Today*, 24 April. Retrieved from https://usatoday.com/story/news/world/2018/04/24/toronto-van-attack-suspect-alek-minassian/544944002.

nazianime (2020). "This is who various 'incels' in our community are trying to bring in to the community." *Incels.co*, 8 August. Retrieved from https://incels.co/threads/this-is-who-various-incels-in-our-community-are-trying-to-bring-in-to-the-community.230048/.

Theweleit, Klaus (1977) [1987]. *Male Fantasies Volume One: Women, Floods, Bodies, History*. Minneapolis: University of Minnesota Press.

15. Naming Things

Steven Ramey

Words matter. Which words we use to describe a person or a group can have a significant impact on the image that our description and analysis constructs. Coming one month after the Parkland School shooting in February 2018, a ceremony in Pennsylvania that involved the blessing of AR-15s drew considerable response in the traditional media and across social media. For example, an NPR headline read "AR-15s Are Biblical 'Rod Of Iron' at Pennsylvania Church" above a photo of people, primarily women, dressed in white (Neuman 2018). The woman at the front wore a crown and had a rifle in one hand while raising the other hand in the air. It is easy to see the ways that the narrative about the ceremony became a pawn within the renewed (again) gun control debate, as it illustrates how the presentation of events and facts are more about the interests of those interpreting and presenting them than the specifics of the events or details. But more than that point (which my colleagues have made in other chapters in this volume, such as Martha Smith's "Is There Neo-Nazi DNA?" and Jason W. M. Ellsworth's "Marketing the Authentic Taco") is the significance of the names that different commentators used for this group and ceremony.

Headlines on CBS News and NPR, among others, described the event as occurring in a Pennsylvania church (CBS News 2018; Neuman 2018). Whatever the intent of the respective editors, some on social media used the ritual as evidence of a problematic commitment to guns among (presumably) conservative American Christians. Newsweek used an alternative label in the headline, identifying the ceremony as a ritual within a cult (though the web address retained the church label) (Sit 2018). While naming the organization a "church" provides a certain authenticity for the group in a culture historically dominated by Christianity, the reference to a cult generates the opposite, a sense of being inauthentic that can produce a subsequent reaction of fear of illegitimate fringe groups fueled by what people assume are radical, irrational commitments.

Which classification is more accurate is not my primary concern, as various groups use the different labels (for themselves and others) to promote their own legitimacy and social interests. The bigger question is how do commentators decide when to accept a group's or individual's self-identification as authentic and when to replace those self-identifications with an alternative. The organization that conducted this blessing of AR-15s identifies as both the World Peace and Unification Sanctuary and the shortened Sanctuary Church. An offshoot of the Unification Church that is sometimes labeled the "Moonies," the organization follows the leadership of a married couple, Revs. Hyung Jin Moon and Yeon Ah Lee Moon, who, according to the group's website, are "carrying on the providential work of his father, the Rev. Sun Myung Moon, whose encounter with Jesus at age fifteen led to his six-decade worldwide ministry to fulfill Christ's mission, based on the Bible and the Divine Principle" ("Welcome" 2018). While they do not specifically use the term "Christian" for themselves, the organization uses the terms church, ministry, Bible, and Christ's mission, much as other groups who identify as Christian do. Thus, based on self-identification, the name church is accurate.

As much as the organization probably benefits if seen as a legitimate part of global churches, others choose to ignore that name, replacing it with the term "cult" as a means to marginalize the group and its teachings that diverge in places from those of many groups that identify as Christian. Other groups, such as the Southern Poverty Law Center (SPLC), use the label cult when describing certain ideas of the Sanctuary Church that these groups oppose, such as what the SPLC names as its racism, anti-Semitism, and anti-LGBT positions (Kelley 2018).

Seeing how various groups use different terms for the organization as much (if not more) to further their own preferences and ideas as to present an accurate description, anyone discussing the organization, whether scholars or journalists or random people on Facebook,

94 *Fabricating Authenticity*

choose what name to use, and in that choice, whether intentionally or not, promote one of a variety of positions. It is not sufficient to repeat the name that a group uses for itself, as others who use that same label will probably contest that name. Ignoring the group's self-identification for the preferences of their opponents is no better. Unless we choose to enter into the debate over what constitutes acceptable Christianity, the best alternatives are to either avoid the debate with a neutral label (organization, ceremony, etc.) or highlight whose labeling is being repeated (e.g., a group that identifies as a church, a cult according to its detractors). Of course, such neutrality and precision is also important when discussing mainstream groups. Only contextualizing the names of marginal groups reinforces, without sufficient critique and contextualization, the dichotomy between mainstream and marginal. Because the name (and its associated connotations) makes a significant difference, such precise acknowledgement of whose label we use when naming things is vital to avoid playing favorites unintentionally.

Steven Ramey is Professor and Chair in the Department of Religious Studies at the University of Alabama, where he also is Director of Asian Studies. He is author of *Hindu, Sufi, or Sikh* (Palgrave, 2008) and editor of several volumes. His most recent project is the co-written *Religions of the World: Questions, Challenges, and New Directions* (Equinox Publishing Ltd., 2024) with Leslie Dorrough Smith.

References

Kelley, Brendan Joel (2018). "Anti-LGBT Cult Leader Calls on Followers to Purchase Assault Rifles." *Southern Poverty Law Center*, 9 February. Retrieved from https://www.splcenter.org/hatewatch/2018/02/09/anti-lgbt-cult-leader-calls-followers-purchase-assault-rifles (accessed 28 March 2018).

CBS News (2018). "Hundreds Gather at Church for Blessing Ceremony Featuring AR-15s." *CBS News*, 28 February. Retrieved from https://www.cbsnews.com/news/hundreds-of-worshipers-gather-at-church-hosting-ceremony-featuring-ar-15s/ (accessed 28 March 2018).

Neuman, Scott (2018). "AR-15s Are Biblical 'Rod Of Iron' At Pennsylvania Church." *NPR*, 1 March. Retrieved from https://www.npr.org/sections/thetwo-way/2018/03/01/589808670/ar-15s-are-biblical-rod-of-iron-at-pennsylvania-church (accessed 28 March 2018).

Sit, Ryan (2018). "'Cult' Heir Hosts 'Blessing' Ceremony Featuring AR-15s, Causes Nearby School to Relocate Students for Safety." *Newsweek*, 26 February. Retrieved from https://www.newsweek.com/ar-15-church-ceremony-moonies-cult-school-shooting-parkland-florida-820465 (accessed 28 March 2018).

"Welcome" (2018). *World Peace and Unification Sanctuary*. Retrieved from https://www.sanctuary-pa.org/ (accessed 28 March 2018).

16. While Whitey's on the Moon

Annie Rose O'Brien

To repeat Steven Ramey's opening statement, words matter. The words we use, and the feelings they evoke, have serious consequences in shaping how we understand a particular topic, a particular person, or a particular desire. Words create networks, relationships, connections; they also create distance, separation, disconnection, and discord.

We are never removed from the implications, histories, and legacies of words. A word, a phrase, a sentence, a story—any of these can conjure a particular narrative or understanding of the world that we align ourselves with. I think of this a lot as a graduate student, as someone who reads and writes on race, religion, and the southern United States. As scholars in the field of Religious Studies, we constantly grapple with how religion has been and is defined, by whom and to what end, and the ways in which particular definitions have worked to shape and define our field. Our work is to explore contestations, frictions, and assumptions around what religion is, and what it can be. Often, this work takes us out of the realms of what is considered traditionally "religious," and demonstrates that religion, like so many other social categories, is not so cleanly delineated. Ideas of race, gender, religion, nationalism, history, humanity are all entangled and interwoven in the web of the past and the present. The words we choose to discuss religion, to discuss anything, evoke broader frameworks of understanding and acceptance, as well as division and refusal, and so we are tasked with attentiveness to the stories we hear and choose to tell, as well as the histories we choose to authenticate.

And this is what I have found myself asking: is positioning oneself as neutral or objective desirable, or even possible? If language is always tied to people and places and histories, can it ever truly be neutral? And how does the veneration of neutrality reinforce the power of academia to continue shaping what we consider to be main-stream or marginal?

On July 4, 2020, U.S. President Donald Trump gave a speech from a mountain known by the Lakota Sioux as *Thuŋkášila Šákpe,* or Six Grandfathers. This name was given long before the mountain rock was blasted and carved into the "Shrine of Democracy," known commonly now as Mount Rushmore, and described by the president as "an eternal tribute to our forefathers and to our freedom" (Trump 2020a). Trump stated that "our nation is witnessing a merciless campaign to wipe out our history, defame our heroes, erase our values, and indoctrinate our children" and argued this campaign is composed of totalitarian, far-left fascists wielding "cancel culture" in an attempt to "tear down statues of our Founders, deface our most sacred memorials, and unleash a wave of violent crime in our cities" (ibid.). Trump called for Americans to stand unwavering against "lies meant to divide us, demoralize us, and diminish us," and "go[ing] forward united in our purpose and re-dedicated in our resolve…, we will teach our children to know that they live in a land of legends, that nothing can stop them, and that no one can hold them down" (ibid.).

Trump's framing of what is currently known as the 2020 Uprising evokes a sense of fear, instability, and the necessity for swift action against the potential destruction of America. Protests are labeled as a moral and religious threat to the dominant American mythos and its most-beloved saints and heroes. Trump characterizes the social forces mobilizing protestors as an inauthentic and violent religion: "If you do not speak its language, perform its rituals, recite its mantras, and follow its commandments, then you will be censored, banished, blacklisted, persecuted, and punished" (2020a).

This, of course, is not an unbiased description of what is happening. In a Juneteenth interview, Angela Davis referred to the 2020 Uprising as "an extraordinary moment which has brought together a whole number of [social justice] issues," and created an "opportunity for us to begin to reimagine the meaning of these states" (Mosley and Hagan 2020). Davis connected the moment with broader, ongoing struggles in the U.S. for racial and economic justice, stating it was time to begin the "hard work of creating new institutions" that exist outside of and in opposition to racisms. She also referred to

98 *Fabricating Authenticity*

the Uprising as a collective witnessing of "one of the most brutal examples of state violence," a reference to the reasons behind the federal responses to the ongoing protests. Davis stated, "for hundreds of years Black people have passed down this collective yearning for freedom from one generation to the next. We're doing now what should have been done in the aftermath of slavery" (ibid.).

Davis's framing of recent events prioritizes a different history, one that she claims Trump is "totally ignorant of," and one that continues to shape and divide people in the present (Mosley and Hagan 2020). While Trump argues that no one can hold Americans down, Davis highlights the countless ways in which Black Americans have been held down—violently, systematically, literally—by their nation. She does not highlight monuments or memorials, but the legacy of racial capitalism that continues in the present. There is still fear, and a sense of America under threat, but these are connected to very different ideas of who and what is under attack, as well as what it would mean for America to fail. Failure comes from the inability of Americans and America to learn and grow from our past, to recognize and address "the ways in which capitalism and racism are interlinked" in the formation and development of this country, and to resist and abolish the colonial logics that continue to shape public understandings and institutions of the present (ibid.). But more than fear, Davis expresses hope and a sense of optimism—in how this moment can help us understand how "our lives are intertwined with those of people all over the world," disrupting an isolated and individualistic sense of American; how we can reject a world "created by capitalism" and imagine new ways of being and living with one another; and how the 2020 election will allow those who are calling for the abolition of prisons as we know them to begin "the hard work of creating new institutions" (ibid.).

Trump's language also promotes a particular understanding of the U.S. and its people. His speech defines Americans as "the people who pursued our Manifest Destiny across the ocean, into the uncharted wilderness, over the tallest mountains, and then into the skies and even into the stars" (2020a). This definition erases any perception of America existing prior to European colonization and shows a complete lack of recognition towards the land from which he made his speech. Colonization or Manifest Destiny? Uncharted wilderness or Native land? The unceded territory of the Lakota Sioux or public lands of the United States? *Thuŋkášila Šákpe* or Six Grandfathers or Mount Rushmore or "an eternal tribute to our forefathers and to our freedom" (ibid.)?

The words we use, and the stories they tell or obscure, matter. When our words and ourselves are connected to broader frameworks of social, religious, and cultural understanding, neutrality is not a possible option or approach; even when chosen carefully, words implicate us in broader structures. As academics, as people, we will always be working to understand and explain the world. It is not always so simple as avoiding favoritism or balancing mainstream and marginal approaches, particularly when many mainstream frameworks and definitions work to reify systems and structures of racial, economic, and colonial oppression.

Some Christians in the U.S. have expressed fear they'll be the next victim of "cancel culture" or that any attack on America is an attack on its Christian foundations and Christianity itself. In a July 19, 2020, interview, Trump stated that, were Joe Biden to be elected, "first of all, he won't call the shots. The people—the radical left people that's around him will call. Religion will be gone, OK? Life, you could forget about that, the whole question of life" (2020b). When pushed to explain the phrase, "religion will be gone," Trump gestured to pandemic social distancing measures: "Well, look at what they're doing to the churches. They won't let the churches even open if they want to stand in a field six feet apart. We've had churches that wanted to stand in fields six feet apart. There has never been an administration that's done so much as I have, from tax cuts to regulation cuts to rebuilding the military to getting choice for the vets. Nobody's done the things I've done. Nobody. In three and a half years no other president's been able to do what I've done" (ibid.). In this iteration, religion is churches, is tax cuts, is military support, is veteran support, is the president, is Trump. The definition grows and grows, until everything is under threat.

Countless histories reduced to rival definitions—a rhetorically effective way to dismiss or delegitimize certain groups or perspectives. Trump declares Antifa a terrorist organization, calls protestors

100   *Fabricating Authenticity*

"thugs," quotes the violent, racist language of Walter Headley ("when the looting starts, the shooting starts"), threatens demonstrators with law and order, and claims what is under attack is nothing less than the history, fabric, and future of America. The ambiguity of these ideas is particularly useful for both reaching a broad audience and naturalizing Trump's perspective as *the* American perspective. Protestors, in a similar appeal to American ideals, express a desire for justice not found in the American legal system, a bone-deep weariness with racism in America, and a necessity to reckon with America's past and reconsider its future.

Riots, Unlawful Assemblies, Looting, Thugs, Radicals, Far-Left Fascists, Terrorists.

Protests, Demonstrations, Rebellions, Peaceful Protestors, Organizers, Advocates, Communities.

The destruction of a certain America and a reimagining of an alternative America.

As an academic and in every other facet of my life/self, I am constantly learning and unlearning and thinking and rethinking the stories I hear and the stories I wish to tell. What is my role in supporting or challenging systems that produce and reproduce the mainstream and the marginal? When do I balance viewpoints, and when do I refuse theoretical debate of tangible, violent realities? Trump states that "no movement that seeks to dismantle these treasured American legacies can possibly have a love of America at its heart" (2020a), but what are those legacies and who gets to define them? What histories do our narratives authorize and what perspectives do our words legitimize? Is "love" defined only in terms of support and veneration, or can "love" push us to have difficult conversations, thoughtful revisions, and expanded understandings?

As academics, as people, these are questions we must answer for ourselves.

Annie Rose O'Brien is an Assistant Professor of Religion at Catawba College in Salisbury, North Carolina. Her work considers race, religion, and public memory in the Southern U.S. through the contemporary memorialization of lynching murder victims and the defacement, removal, destruction, and—more recently—the re-installation of Confederate monuments. She explores how subaltern memory is unearthed in order to contest dominant symbols, narratives, and mythologies of the nation-state, as well as the colonial logics which continue to belie its actions. Her work emphasizes white claims of supremacy as part of a project of spatial domination which seeks to sacralize whiteness through public history, ritual acts, and visual and material culture.

References

Mosley, Tonya, and Allison Hagan (2020). "'An Extraordinary Moment': Angela Davis Says Protests Recognize Long Overdue Anti-Racist Work." *WBUR*, 19 June. Retrieved from https://www.wbur.org/hereandnow/2020/06/19/angela-davis-protests-anti-racism.

Scott-Heron, Gil (1970). "Whitey on the Moon." Track 9 on *Small Talk at 125th and Lenox*. Flying Dutchman/RCA.

Trump, Donald (2020a). "Remarks by President Trump at South Dakota's 2020 Mount Rushmore Fireworks Celebration." *The White House*, 4 July. Retrieved from https://trumpwhitehouse.archives.gov/briefings-statements/remarks-president-trump-south-dakotas-2020-mount-rushmore-fireworks-celebration-keystone-south-dakota/.

———. (2020b). "Transcript: 'Fox News Sunday' Interview with President Trump" (Chris Wallace, Interviewer). *Fox News*, 19 July. Retrieved from https://www.foxnews.com/politics/transcript-fox-news-sunday-interview-with-president-trump.

17. In Their Own Terms

Vaia Touna

One of my upper-level seminars is on "Theorizing Ancient Greek Religion" where we discuss the anachronistic uses of categories that scholars use, such as "religion," in describing and therefore understanding the past and most specifically ancient Greece, reading among other things Brent Nongbri's book, *Before Religion: A History of a Modern Concept* (2013). For those not familiar with the book, Nongbri offers a historical study of the category religion, tracing its origins not to the ancient world but to modern Europe. When used to describe ancient practices, Nongbri suggests that the term is anachronistically projected backwards in time (in fact, many other scholars have also found the use of the word religion to be problematic in reading ancient material—despite the fact that, and ironically perhaps, some still go on to use it all the same!), urging his readers to be at the very least self-aware when they use that word to talk about the past.

Now, my students, as a final assignment, are usually asked to find examples where they see similar moves happening elsewhere, that is, anachronism used to talk about the past. All the students, prior to writing their final assignments, have to present in class the example that they are working on in order to get feedback from their peers. They all came up with wonderful examples, from Morgan Freeman's search for the Afterlife (a National Geographic documentary), and university campus tours, to church restorations, Disney animated films, and even to a modern illuminated, handwritten Bible that was commissioned by Saint John's University—a Bible that was described on the Library of Congress's site as "at once old and new" (2015).

One of the examples that was presented in class struck a particular nerve in me. It was the 2000 crime comedy film *O Brother, Where Art Thou?* written, produced, and directed by the Coen brothers.

The movie is set in the 1930s US South, and tells the story of a convict, played by George Clooney, who, along with two other inmates, escapes prison to get back to his wife and home—a movie that, as we learn from the opening credits, is based on Homer's poem, *Odyssey* (2003).

Why this example was of particular interest to me is because I remember the first time that I saw the movie, several years ago, and recalled that describing the ancient world, for me at least, relied heavily on the idea of understanding that world "in its own terms." Although I liked the movie (in part, I should be honest, because who doesn't like a George Clooney singing "I am a Man of Constant Sorrow" [even if not with his own voice!!]), I admit that I was quite disappointed about the way the myth of Odysseus was represented, that is, I felt it was yet another American movie that "distorted" an ancient Greek myth, something that certainly spoke of my own cultural sensibilities at the time (given my own upbringing and schooling in Greece), and thus my sense for how ancient Greek myths *ought to* be told.

Now, during our class discussion, all of the examples were evidently understood as modern, and that the creators of the movie, for example, were seen as constructing something new by using something old, and so, of course, they were not trying to understand or describe, for example, the myth of Odysseus in its own terms—all this was very obvious to the class. Even if in the case of the illuminated manuscript the commentator suggests, that, "the contemporary bible is at once old and new" it was obvious to us that it was contemporary, something explicitly evident in its very modern artistic representations. All the examples, therefore, even if they made reference, in one way or another, to the past, were seen as primarily influenced by the cultures from which they emerged, and, of course, seen also in light of their intended modern audience.

But the examples also presented us with the opportunity to think about and challenge the things that we do not so easily understand as equally modern and situated within a specific historical period, with its own discourses and interests; mainly I have in mind scholarly descriptions and interpretations of past materials that are disguised under such common phrases as, for example, "understanding them

104   *Fabricating Authenticity*

in their own terms." Certainly when I saw that Coen brothers' movie for the first time, as someone who was trained in the history of religions and studied the ancient world, I acted without much thinking as an authority on the material, who was able to judge the liberties of the film makers as *mis*representing the myth and thus failing to keep up with the "original," the "authentic" version. I think it is the same when using the phrase "in its own terms" for, although commonly used, it helps us to naturalize and thereby authorize new scholarly vocabulary and schemata that critique and replace the descriptions and interpretations of a previous generation of scholars. The phrase then makes possible a scholarly move that shifts the attention from the author and her/his interests in their present—deriving from her/his theoretical questions and methods—and from her or his intended audience, and, instead, places emphasis on the object or the people one studies as if they are the authentic source of meaning, a meaning that predates the interpreter and the descriptor. The challenge, though, is to see the contemporaneity and historicity of every description and every interpretation as itself being a modern act, whether in a movie, illuminated manuscript, art restoration or even a scholarly work.

When it comes to reading "religion" in the ancient world what I find particularly interesting, then, is that even when scholars are adamant about the need to understand the ancient world "in its own terms," thereby urging us on contextualizing and going to the primary sources in order to accurately describe it, they seem to be taking liberties similar to the artistic liberties of the Coen brothers, by projecting seemingly innocent modern terms as self-evidently appearing in the ancient data which they often describe as "religious" (think of all those "religious" ceremonies and stories and sacrifices that we all just know the ancient Greeks supposedly had). This prompts one, rightly, I think, to ask a question: in whose "own terms" are such scholars describing and then analyzing the ancient material? For it seems that "in their own terms" is a rhetorical move on the part of current scholars that implicitly, yet effectively it seems, authorize *the authenticity of their own work*. With this otherwise seemingly sincere and innocent move, one that supposedly gives voice to those who don't have one any longer, it's the scholar's own voice that gets to be the guarantor of how a text, material artefact or even a people, past or present, should be read and therefore understood.

In other words, the challenge is to take seriously our own historicity and positionality and to be explicit of (and thus owning our) scholarly liberties, such as "in *our* own terms," for the purpose of working through *our* own curiosities, all in the service of understanding the world in which *we* are now living—a world that we continually help to make by our talking about people long gone. What studying anachronism therefore invites us to do is to take seriously that the way we talk about the world, present or past, speaks primarily of our own scholarly interests, positions, situations, cultural sensibilities as well as the intended audiences to which we are writing or talking.

This is definitely a challenge of constant sorrows for anyone working with ancient (or should I now say always contemporary) artefacts, a challenge that is surprisingly similar to Odysseus' adventures and efforts to get back to Ithaca, but perhaps we should be less concerned about the destination and more about the trip—that is, our theories and methods (paraphrasing Constantine Cavafy's poem "Ithaca" [1911]). Besides even Odysseus never really returned to the Ithaca he once left from.

Vaia Touna is Associate Professor in the Department of Religious Studies at the University of Alabama, Tuscaloosa. She is author of *Fabrications of the Greek Past: Religion, Tradition, and the Making of Modern Identities* (Brill, 2017) and editor of *Strategic Acts in the Study of Identity: Towards a Dynamic Theory of People and Place* (Equinox Publishing Ltd., 2019). Her research interests focus on the sociology of religion, acts of identification and social formation, historiography, as well as theoretical and methodological issues concerning the study of "religion" in the ancient Graeco-Roman world.

References

Cavafy, Constantine P. (1911). "Ithaca." In *C. P. Cavafy Poems 1905–1915*. Greece: Kasimatis & Ionas Printing House.
Coen, Ethan, and Joel Coen, dirs. (2000). *O Brother, Where Art Thou?* Touchstone Pictures and Universal Pictures.

106 *Fabricating Authenticity*

Homer (2003). *The Odyssey*. Trans. E. V. Rieu and D. C. H. Rieu. London: Penguin Books Ltd.

Nongbri, Brent (2013). *Before Religion: A History of a Modern Concept.* New Haven and London: Yale University Press.

Saint John Apostle Bible (2015). Photograph. *Library of Congress.* Washington, D.C. Library of Congress. https://blogs.loc.gov/law/2015/10/modern-illuminated-manuscript-pic-of-the-week/.

18. Shaking a Buddhist House of Cards

Julia Oppermann

Reflecting on the anachronistic use of the category "religion" is, as Touna discusses, an ongoing challenge in the academic study of religion. This is, in part, due to the expectations placed upon us as scholars, but more importantly, it is also *the* central question of our field—the question that follows us everywhere, even when we leave our academic bubble. "In today's world, what even is religion?" And when people hear the words, "I am a scholar of the study of religion," many, understandably, expect me to provide a clear-cut, authoritative answer. Yet, this is a riddle plaguing our entire academic field. Unfortunately—or, I might rather say fascinatingly—I cannot provide a precise answer to that question because any seemingly stable definition implicitly includes preconceived notions of what religion "truly is" based on one's own experiences and perspectives. There is a fine line between the questions "What is religion?" and "Is this (authentic) religion?", so, as scholars of the study of religion, it is our task to consider what is at stake when those questions arise.

Sometimes we ostensibly know exactly *what* religion is, or better, if *that* is religion. Within a specific framework, it may seem like there is nothing to discuss. For example, when speaking about any of the "Big Five," many people might claim that it is an undeniable fact that Christianity, Judaism, Islam, Hinduism, and Buddhism are religions. Although it is sometimes debated whether it is more accurate to describe the last one as a philosophy or a lifestyle, it is nonetheless part of the group we call "world religions" (Masuzawa 2005; Prebish 2019). Many European students learn this at some point in their Religious Education classes in school, and even some undergraduate

108   *Fabricating Authenticity*

programs implicitly follow this approach. In the academic study of religion, students often learn about Christianity, Islam, Judaism, Hinduism, and Buddhism as if they are clearly defined categories referring to equally distinct sets of practices and beliefs (Cotter and Robertson 2016). Slowly, we build a house of cards based on our understanding of what Buddhism is, or, more importantly perhaps, what it is *not*. Our "Buddhism" cards might include meditation, the four noble truths, mindfulness, chanting, and more. Each card in this house represents a realm of knowledge that legitimizes Buddhism as a religion. With each card, the construction grows, establishing a tower of information that seemingly represents "Buddhism." But we should never forget that this is exactly what it is: a construction built by us based on our questions and interests. No matter how stable we think our design is, something can always shake this house of cards.

For example, at the end of 2022, a story about a group of Buddhist monks in Thailand made the headlines of dozens of big newspapers and networks, like *BBC News* (2022) and *The Washington Post*. It eventually also reached the media in my home country, Germany (Welt 2022). One headline read, "Thai Buddhist temple left empty after all its monks test positive for meth" (Watcharasakwej and Pietsch 2022). Sadly, stories about drug abuse have become quite common today, so what is it about this particular story that makes it so compelling? The astonishment arises from the collision of the two allegedly incompatible pieces of information "Thai Buddhist monks" and "meth"—categories that we have been socialized to understand as generally unrelated. The immediate disbelief and confusion from this ostensibly paradoxical headline may even create a sense of amusement. The almost oxymoronic nature of these keywords presents humorous value for American stand-up comedian Josh Johnson, who used this example as a basis for one of his routines in August 2024, when he summarized the seeming hilarity by noting that "It's hard to conceptualize a methy monk!" (Johnson 2024).

But what really makes this incident so hard to conceptualize? Although our Buddhist house of cards is built with cards such as "Thailand" and "monks" that are probably quite secure in our paper construction, the idea of "meth" does not appear to belong. So now, we have two options. One is to try to incorporate it, even if the attempt risks the collapse of the house. Or, two is to ignore this card altogether and cast it aside as an anomaly. For the latter option, we need to find arguments as to why the card should not become a part of our construction. Since number two is the safer option, it is easier to go down this path. The straightforward explanation of why the story of these "methy monks" should not be considered part of Buddhism is because they are not real Buddhists, that is, to consider them as *inauthentic.* Even the local authorities engaged in this discursive boundary policing when they "discussed inviting a 'good monk' from elsewhere to fill in" while the others were in rehab (Watcharasakwej and Pietsch 2022).

So let us look behind this claim of inauthenticity. A key aspect here concerns the perceptions we hold about modernity and ancient lifestyles, which are typically viewed as separate realms. According to the information on our cards, Buddhist monks would appear to live independently of modernity. This is visibly expressed by their "traditional" clothing, homes, and temples that either look or are potentially thousands of years old. A quick analysis of the pictures from the newspaper articles mentioned above shows that the media continually reproduces these fabricated notions of how Buddhists should act and appear. The articles are accompanied by a colorful, exemplary picture of a group of men with short hair wearing orange robes and sitting in prayer. Sometimes, they are atmospherically illuminated by yellow candlelight, as if even the presence of electricity endangers the mystical view of an ancient practice and, thus, the integrity of our Buddhist house of cards. Given how Buddhism is represented, the type of drug used in this incident is of high significance to the narrative. Methamphetamine is a synthetic drug produced in a complicated chemical process that is only possible through the advancement of science in the 19th and 20th centuries. The card in our tower labeled "methamphetamine" thus implicitly challenges the assumption that Buddhism is and will always be an ancient religion, immune to the atrophy of modernity.

Thinking back to Touna's argument, it is interesting that even the responses to the above example label the actions of the Buddhist monks as inauthentic because they do not neatly fit into the house of cards we built. As Johnson also explains,

110 *Fabricating Authenticity*

> when you think of a monk ... you think of someone who has dedicated their entire life ... their physical self, their spiritual well-being to the cause of whatever religion ... they've taken up.... That doesn't make them perfect, but it does make them seem like someone who's going to be holy or be grounded. (2024)

Here, Johnson illustrates that some of those implicit assumptions about Buddhist monks being inherently "good" or "holy"—concepts lacking any universal, stable meaning—which seemingly separate them from modern society and its troubles. In other words, we are projecting an anachronistic idea of a Buddhism of the past and applying it to present-day realities.

But whenever our taken-for-granted structures are challenged, or we intuitively try to safeguard them by dismissing something as being inauthentic, we might, instead, profit from taking a step back and paying closer attention to the dynamics at play. When we see such claims of authenticity at work, it is important to understand that the decision to include or exclude specific cards is always a conscious decision by the builder—it does not matter if it is constructed by a student, a scholar of the study of religion, or any person interested in religion. Religion as a category is always subject to change from within and outside. Our house of cards will never be complete. It will always be unstable and in a state of flux, under constant reconstruction. At times, we may need the house to scientifically work with the idea of religion in specific surroundings. However, we must acknowledge that it is simply a cognitive construction, employed in discrete contexts for particular purposes, and that it is never an authentic reflection of reality. Rather, we might ask if it is our job to work on the building of the house or to analyze why and how it was built in the first place.

Julia Oppermann is an MA student in the Religion in the Public Sphere program at Leibniz University Hannover, Germany, where she also works as the program's social media manager. Her master's thesis examines discourses of alternative medicine in Germany and how the category of "religion" is used to delegitimize such practices from the larger field of medicine. Her further research interests focus on new religious movements and on the interconnection of religion and law in modern societies.

References

BBC News (2022). "Thai monks fail drug tests leaving temple empty." *BBC News*, 29 November 2022. Retrieved from https://www.bbc.com/news/world-asia-china-63792923 (accessed 28 August 2024).

Cotter, Christopher R., and David G. Robertson (2016). "Introduction: The World Religions Paradigm in Contemporary Religious Studies." In Cotter, Christopher R., and David G. Robertson (eds.), *After World Religions. Reconstructing Religious Studies*, 1–20. London and New York: Routledge. https://doi.org/10.4324/9781315688046

Johnson, Josh (2024). "The Demure Trend Explained (Internet's Latest Obsession)." Directed by Jacob Menache. YouTube video, 24:15. Posted 21 August 2024. Retrieved from https://www.youtube.com/watch?v=7EPnT3Txrxs (accessed 27 August 2024).

Masuzawa, Tomoko (2005). *The Invention of World Religions: Or, How European Universalism Was Preserved in the Language of Pluralism.* Chicago: University of Chicago Press.

Prebish, Charles (2019). "Is Buddhism a Religion?" *Lion's Roar*, 4 January. Retrieved from https://www.lionsroar.com/is-buddhism-a-religion/ (accessed 28 August 2024).

Watcharasakwej, Wilawan, and Bryan Pietsch (2022). "Thai Buddhist temple left empty after all its monks test positive for meth." *The Washington Post*, 1 December. Retrieved from https://www.washingtonpost.com/world/2022/12/01/buddhist-monks-drug-tests-thailand-temple/ (accessed 28 August 2024).

Welt (2022). "Alle Mönche positiv auf Meth getestet – Tempel in Thailand verwaist." *Welt*, 30 November. Retrieved from https://www.welt.de/kmpkt/article242409981/Thailand-Tempel-verwaist-Moenche-positiv-auf-Chrystal-Meth-getestet.html (accessed 1 September 2024).

19. "A Good Fake or a Bad Fake?"

Andie Alexander

In the summer of 2012, memes of the seemingly ruined Spanish fresco *Ecce Homo*—also known colloquially as "Potato Jesus" (2012)—took over the internet. Perhaps you recall the story of Cecilia Giménez's attempt to restore the flaky, deteriorating fresco depicting Jesus in a crown of thorns—originally painted by Elías García Martínez—at Sanctuary of Mercy church in Borja, Spain. The "botched restoration" was described as "probably the worst art restoration project of all time," and the local authorities in Borja considered taking legal action against Giménez despite her having worked with approval from the clergy (Minder 2012). The local and global responses—however amusing or critical—policing the purity or authenticity of artwork and restorations highlight the contested and constructed nature of such claims.

Concerns over the authenticity of artwork are particularly important for museum curators seeking to acquire artists' original works; however, museums continue to discover forgeries among their collections. In one recent instance, the Museé Terrus—a museum dedicated to the work of local artist Étienne Terrus—in Elne, France discovered during a renovation that "82 of the 140 pieces in the collection were counterfeits" (Peltier and Codrea-Rado 2018). This museum is not alone in its discovery, so it is not surprising that there are a number of techniques—ranging from ultraviolet fluorescence and optical microscopes to radiocarbon dating and peptide mass fingerprinting—for detecting art forgeries (Schlackman 2018).

Similarly, on the other side of these concerns, there is extensive research and training for "proper" art restoration—i.e., the cleaning, repairing, and painting maintenance for restoring a piece of art to its so-called original appearance. One can see examples of these techniques on TV series such as *The Repair Shop*, where skilled artists and tradespeople demonstrate the processes for repairing and restoring vintage family heirlooms ranging from furniture and clocks to pottery and paintings. In some instances, they restore the heirloom to how it's presumed to have appeared originally, but often, the restorations intentionally maintain certain chosen "flaws" that would demonstrate the life and history of the piece while repairing other signs of wear and tear (Borland 2017).

Other organizations, such as Baumgartner Fine Art Restoration (BFAR), work with museums, art galleries, and government organizations (to name a few) in art conservation and restoration. According to their website, the restorations "alter the artwork as little as possible with respect to the original intention of the artist" and are tailored specifically to the paintings ("About" n.d.). They provide a video of their restoration of *Mother Mary* to demonstrate the processes from cleaning and reframing to touching up and preserving (Baumgartner Restoration 2018). This work—not unlike that of a successful forgery—requires knowledge of what types of paints and canvas were used in different historical periods, and as such, restorers implement a variety of tools to achieve an authentic-looking restoration.

But as I was watching the video, I began to wonder when restorations are considered to be "good" or "necessary" and when they are considered to be destructive. Professional restorations may appear more similar to how we imagine the original piece, but the deteriorated painting may have lost a crucial play of light or shadows. So how are art restorers able to reflect the *original* intention of the artist? And how might we even go about ascertaining an artist's *true* intentions? For the art purist—perhaps even for the art historian—when does the notion of authenticity allow for some leeway? BFAR certainly took great care to match the colors and style of *Mother Mary*, but the finished restoration is not the "original" painting; it's just an attempt at depicting it. The restoration was refurbished with modern tools, paints, chemicals (though some other restorations do use historic materials) that were not present or available at the time the artwork was created.

While the quality of the restored *Mother Mary* may be considered far and above that of *Ecce Homo*, neither is unchanged. This isn't an

114 *Fabricating Authenticity*

argument for authenticity or lack thereof, but rather an observation of when and how claims of authenticity are employed. After all, there is an entire profession focused on art restoration—let alone, art conservation—which provides services to museums and private collectors, so concerns of authenticity extend beyond the art itself (whatever that may be) to economic, social, and cultural concerns.

So the question is: Are these pieces still authentic now that the original has been altered? Is the deteriorated painting which has flaked due to exposure and moisture, been torn and punctured, and gathered dust and grime considered to be more "authentic" before restoration? Or is it just a painting that needs to be restored to appear as we think it would have when initially painted? Considering the profession of art restorers, it would seem that a restored painting is deemed more authentic (read: valuable, perhaps?). The issue then seems to be less concerned with "authenticity" and more about the art's perceived similarity to the so-called original, which makes *claims* of authenticity possible to begin with. Such claims make the world of art and museums possible, establish high culture from low, and commodify those differences.

These debates on art and authenticity remind me of Orson Welles' 1975 *F for Fake*, a film about art fakes and forgery. The film follows the work of Elmyr de Hory, a well-known Hungarian painter and art forger, and probes at notions of truth, art, and trickery. Talking with de Hory about the many forgeries he sold to museums around the world, Welles challenges understandings of experts and authority by suggesting that, like truth or art, such stories and claims are fabricated. Fabrication—recalling Jonathan Z. Smith's argument— "means both to build and to lie" (2013: 15). The fabrication of both art and authenticity depends on the effectiveness of the narrative. As de Hory himself argued, "If you hang [the forgeries] in a museum or collection of your great paintings, and if they hang there long enough, they become real" (Welles 1975). After all, the forgeries hanging on the museum walls are the Picassos or Modiglianis that the public pay to see.

While neither *Mother Mary* nor *Ecce Homo* are forgeries, neither are they unaltered pieces. However, one restoration is presented as a recovery of the original artwork and the other is seen as irrevocably destroyed. Authenticity, then, appears to have less to do with whether a piece is, in fact, exactly as it was (i.e., original) and more to do with how it appears despite alterations. So long as it is similar enough, we can ignore the modern adaptations and corrections to something where they didn't exist previously so long as they don't draw too much attention (Alexander 2013)—or, more importantly, detract from the determined value of the piece. To use the language of Welles, the authenticity of these restorations lies in the success of their fabrication. Or, as argued by Clifford Irving in *F for Fake*: "The important distinction to make, when you're talking about the genuine quality of a painting, is not so much whether it's a real painting or a fake: It's whether it's a good fake or a bad fake."

Andie Alexander is a doctoral candidate in the Institute for the Study of Religion at Leibniz University Hannover and is Managing Editor of *The Religious Studies Project*. Her research focuses on identity construction, discourses of difference and experience, and conceptions of the individual as a way of examining how post-9/11 discourses of inclusivity and pluralism implicitly work as a form of governance and subject-making which construct and constrain the liberal Muslim subject.

References

"About" (n.d.). *Baumgartner Fine Art Restoration*. Retrieved from https://baumgartnerfineartrestoration.com/about.shtml (accessed 2 December 2018).

Alexander, Andie (2013). "Mind the Gap," *Studying Religion in Culture* (blog), 24 September. Retrieved from https://religion.ua.edu/blog/2013/09/24/mind-the-gap/ (accessed 2 December 2018).

Baumgartner Restoration (2018). "The Restoration of Mother Mary Narrated." YouTube video, 08:00. Posted 17 September 2018. Retrieved from https://www.youtube.com/watch?v=ON7mhkSwTIk&vl=es-419/ (accessed 2 December 2018).

Borland, Ben, dir. (2017). *The Repair Shop*. Ricochet. BBC One and BBC Two.

Minder, Rafael (2012). "Despite Good Intentions, a Fresco in Spain Is Ruined." *The New York Times*, 24 August. Retrieved from https://

116 *Fabricating Authenticity*

www.nytimes.com/2012/08/24/world/europe/botched-restoration-of-ecce-homo-fresco-shocks-spain.html/ (accessed 2 December 2018).

Peltier, Elian, and Anna Codrea-Rado (2018). "French Museum Discovers More Than Half Its Collection is Fake." *The New York Times*, 30 April. Retrieved from https://www.nytimes.com/2018/04/30/arts/design/french-museum-fakes.html/ (accessed 13 December 2019).

"Potato Jesus" (2012). *Know Your Meme*. Retrieved from https://knowyourmeme.com/memes/potato-jesus (accessed 2 December 2018).

Schlackman, Steve (2018). "These Techniques Can Detect Art Forgery." *Artrepreneur: Art Law Journal*, 3 May. Retrieved from https://artrepreneur.com/journal/detecting-art-forgeries/ (accessed 2 December 2018).

Smith, Jonathan Z. (2013). "The Introductory Course: Less is Better." In Christopher I. Lehrich (ed.), *On Teaching Religion*, 11–19. Oxford: Oxford University Press. https://doi.org/10.1093/acprof:os obl/9780199944293.003.0002

Welles, Orson, dir. (1975). *F for Fake*. Janus Films.

20. Pay Attention!: Media, Performance, and Discourses on Authenticity

Daniel Jones

Andie Alexander's study of art and authenticity introduces us to the pitfalls of unchecked assumptions regarding religion's origins, authenticity, and essences as mediated by restorations. I want to bridge this important consideration with another: religious performance (e.g., prayers, rituals, meals, etc.). Performance scholars caution us from separating things like plays, dance, and street art, from everyday performances using rhetoric such as the "mundane" or "sacred"—especially in "religious" ritual (Schechner 2004). Such scholars have also debated cultural authenticity in ritual itself (DuBois et al. 2011; Chidester 2003). Building on this line of thinking, I argue for the importance of shifting our focus to the *performance* of "authenticity" by both participants and observers. As changes or alterations to artwork may, for some, reflect a shift in authenticity, changes in social and performative behaviors during certain rituals may have a similar impact on others.

Consider, for a moment, which media objects (e.g., sacred texts, audio-visual aides in translating sacred discourse, statues, even bodies and environments) are regarded as authentic in any given religious ceremony. Do certain technologies, media or otherwise, disrupt an observer's trust in the authenticity of certain ritual performances? If so, what informs those distinctions? Despite the increase in "new media" and the use of mobile technologies among religious communities, the role of media and technology in religious events remains contested (Taru 2019). Building on Alexander's analysis of the ways in which visual and technological methods of art restoration impact

118 *Fabricating Authenticity*

conceptions of authenticity, I argue that performances and media understood as "religious" can also incite contests over authenticity. I am further taking as my point of departure here the idea that people co-evolve with their technologies, and as such, any discourses on the authenticity of human actions when using any forms of technologies (including media) have implications for how to talk about, conceive, and discipline what it means to be human (Hayles 2012).

For example, in 2019, Charismatic preacher Perry Stone, who formerly worked with Voice of Evangelism ministries in Cleveland, TN, was filmed checking his phone while purportedly speaking in tongues (Glossolalia). The video, in which Stone's utterances noticeably change in intonation while he checks his mobile phone, went viral, and there were a number of responses claiming the pastor's performance of a Charismatic rite was disingenuous. The story broke on the blog, *Friendly Atheist* (Mehta 2019a) but was quickly picked up by other outlets, such as DeadState (Palma 2019). In analyzing reactions from observers and blog commentators on social media, I argue that claims of what gets to count as "authentic religion" or "authentic religious expression" (and therefore, "inauthentic") are necessarily informed by understandings of media and attention—terms which, like religion, are themselves contested. Thus far, there is no definitive information about what the pastor was looking at on his phone, but public responses from a range of parties identifying within and without (Charismatic) Christianity reflect a skepticism about what content could have legitimated his interaction with a smart phone—a media technology—during the sermon. While one can search "Perry Stone," "phone," and "speaking in tongues" on any major social media sites and find many personal accounts (interestingly, from my experience, accounts belonging to both scholars and non-scholars) with analogous language, a tweet from the Twitter account @Protestia offers an example: "[Checking his phone] would be funny … if it weren't blasphemy of the Holy Ghost" (Protestia 2019). Reactions might have been different if the attention-grabbing object was, say, a book—another media technology such as the Bible. Objects of media and technology garner identities within ritual settings just as do people. Changes to the presence, use, and form of media and technology within ritual settings, as Alexander demonstrated, are subject to audience expectations. Moreover, it is interesting to note how certain changes affect ritual *attention*, and how the affecting of attention impacts sentiments of authenticity.

These exceptions are also present in how and where certain objects and performances are authorized when they are understood to follow the expectations for the event. For example, we might understand the bible as an object, a prop (using performance studies terminology), that, regardless of whether the pastor actually reads from it, has been legitimized historically. Mobile phones, apps, and social media, however, are considered "new media" objects, which may or may not be used as e-book bibles, and these objects are commonly understood to be a distraction (e.g., people are often asked to silence and put away their phones while in class, a religious service, or a movie). Would the reaction of observers be the same if folks knew that he accessed an e-bible? One may ask whether, or rather, *how* that matters, but given that virtually all observers of Stone had no knowledge of what, exactly, was on his phone, we can see how their reactions to these performances reveal more about their expectations and assumptions about the use of certain technologies and media in "sacred" rituals than they can reveal any sort of "authenticity" of performance.

From this example, we also can begin to see how *attention* functions as a legitimating aspect of "religious performances," and therefore, "religious authenticity" because Stone's perceived *in*attention marked his performance as *in*authentic. Attention, in this sense, is understood to be a crucial component because it demarcates the "authentic religious experience" from an otherwise mundane activity. Expanding this analysis of authenticity to that of attention, we can explore how understandings of attention (and consequently, inattention) often rely on taken-for-granted ideas about "normal" or "standard" neurological processes, or neuronormativity. So, what might be the consequences for those whose life conditions are shaped by neurological conditions that affect certain performances of attention? Are they no longer able to be "authentically religious?" Specifically, what sort of assumptions about attention inform popular understandings of "authentic religion?" To address this, I invite you to consider claims of "authentic attention" that are implicitly informed by neuronormative ideologies.

120   *Fabricating Authenticity*

Regarding the conflict over the phone, we see two converging dynamics: the authorized media technologies of religious performance (e.g., the Bible), which are negotiated between performers and audiences, and authorized performances (e.g., neuronormative behaviors) of ritual attention. The acceptance of *authorized media and technology* as conducive of "authentic religious behavior" implicitly establishes a standard by which social so-called religious performances are measured. For example, the pastor could have a condition which affects his executive functioning, such as Attention Deficit Hyperactivity Disorder (ADHD), but if he did, the audience would likely have no knowledge of this. Moreover, the claim of the pastor's disfluency in Glossolalia asserts that neuronormative attention is demonstrable proof of authenticity, either in belief or divine interaction. In this case, one's religious authenticity is determined by one's cognitive ability, and as such, inattention *or* unauthorized technology usage may become hindrances to a fully authorized performance of "religious experience."

But rather than getting caught up in yet another contest of authenticity, we can step back to examine how these assumptions impact people's standing in religious communities. While deriding observers laughed and scoffed because Stone's performance imitated that of the everyday distracted individual instead of one purportedly in the throes of miraculous communication, their implicit criteria for authenticity may limit inclusion for those with executive function impairments which "hinder" so-called authentic religious performance. Though these implicit criteria may be more focused on delegitimizing Charismatic Christianity as a whole, such ableist rhetoric ultimately—though perhaps inadvertently—reinforces neurological hierarchies. That is, only typical cognitive functioning counts as "authentic religious experience/performance." Such claims of inauthenticity assert that *neuronormative* ritual performances are proof of either authentic religiosity divine communication or authentic belief in such; therefore, by these standards, the religious performer cannot both have a condition which affects their attention and have an authentic religious experience. While I am unaware of any claims that Stone has ADHD or any other neurological condition that would impact his performance of attention, those in religious communities who do have neurological conditions which affect attention will likely feel the exclusion (Hathaway and Barkley 2003). In this way, we can see how authenticity is continually re-constructed, even by one who considers themselves outside of the group subjected to these criteria of authenticity.

Studies show that people with ADHD in church settings feel precarity and insecurity about religious experiences based on attention functioning issues (ibid.). It is further interesting that this discourse of authenticity is negotiated by those who do and do not identify with Charismatic Christianity! The problem of whether or not a critic belongs to a group while doing the criticizing (the "insider/outsider problem" of religious studies) should not obscure how certain religious performances get authenticated or not in any given discourse (McCutcheon 1999). It is, rather, more analytically responsible to ask what the authenticating party has to gain from authenticating rhetoric.

While the curators of the atheist blog that originally sparked debate over the video of Pastor Stone's Glossolalia incident may not identify with Stone's religious identity, they nonetheless present an understanding of "authentic religious experience" which necessitates particular performances of attention. Moreover, in response to Pastor Stone's original religious performance (Mehta 2019b) and subsequent defense video (Perry Stone 2019), a Baptist pastor, Dr. Gene Kim, explicitly criticized Stone's use of a phone as disqualifying Stone's performance as authentic Glossolalia (Real Bible Believers 2019). This carries potentially ableist assumptions that entire attention be required for "sincere" or "authentic" performance of religious rites. How individuals with a range of disabilities perform religion receives attention from both fellow religionist performers and observers (not solely scholars). The rhetorical, ideological construction of sincerity (and, as such, authenticity), not sincerity itself, can be observed.

Ritual and performance space, sensory, and media cultures are structured around gaining and holding audiences' attention on certain ideas, themes, and figures, it is "first and foremost, a mode of paying attention" (Smith 1987: 103). Extreme attention to something is often framed *as religion*, extreme attention to standardization as ritual, and ritual performance as religion. Is, then, the inverse true? Is extreme inattention nonreligion? These theoretical questions may have deeper

122   *Fabricating Authenticity*

implications than space allows to address here. If the pastor's phone operated as a distraction of sorts, does that delegitimize the authenticity of the Glossolalia performance in the eyes of observers? And who gets to determine the authenticity of his performance?

So, one need not defend (or critique) Glossolalia nor the pastor in order to think more critically about the role of media and attention in the way that certain behaviors and performances get coded *as* religion, authentic/sincere, or successful. Rather, reactions to videos such as this reveal how society codes certain objects as "sacred" and "profane," especially while lacking important knowledge about the conditions of their usage. And not unlike claims of "authentic religion," understandings of "attention," as well as the objects associated with it, I argue, require more critical reflection and consideration. Can one have access to things deemed sacred and be distracted? What level of attention constitutes a necessary condition of authentic religion or religious authenticity? What objects may take and hold our attention while still retaining "authenticity?"

Daniel Jones is an independent scholar, editor, writer, and educator whose research focuses on the intersection of religious, environmental, resource extraction, posthumanism, and science and technology discourses. Daniel received an MA in Religious Studies from Missouri State University, and currently co-edits the American Religion section of the journal *Religious Studies Review*.

References

Chidester, David (2003). "Fake Religion: Ordeals of Authenticity in the Study of Religion," *Journal for the Study of Religion* 16/2: 71–97. https://doi.org/10.4314/jsr.v16i2.6111

Du Bois, Fletecher, Eric de Maaker, Karen Polit, and Marianne Riphagen (2011). "From Ritual Ground to Stage." In Ronald Grimes, Ute Hüsken, Udo Simon, and Eric Venbrux (eds.), *Ritual, Media, and Conflict*, 35–62. New York: Oxford University Press. https://doi.org/10.1093/acprof:oso/9780199735235.003.0002

Dyer, John (2019). "The Habits and Hermeneutics of Digital Bible Readers: Comparing Print and Screen Engagement, Comprehension, and

Behavior," *Journal of Religion, Media, and Digital Culture* 8/2: 181–205. https://doi.org/10.1163/21659214-00802001

Hathaway, William L., and Russell A. Barkley (2003). "Self-regulation, ADHD, & Child Religiousness," *Journal of Psychology and Christianity* 22/2: 101–114.

Hayles, Katherine N. (2012). *How We Think: Digital Media and Technogenesis*. Chicago: University of Chicago Press.

McCutcheon, Russell T. (1999). *The Insider/Outsider Problem in the Study of Religion: A Reader*. New York: Continuum.

Mehta, Hemant (2019a). "Watch This Preacher Check His Phone While Speaking in Tongues." *Patheos: Nonreligious: Friendly Atheist*, 28 September. Retrieved from https://friendlyatheist.patheos.com/2019/09/28/watch-this-preacher-check-his-phone-while-speaking-in-tongues/?utm_source=dlvr.it&utm_medium=facebook&fbclid=IwAR1gW-1JYqf_-tfFBq19edJRqsV_Gyq64jiO9PAjRhDQ98WyH1-VKsA0Zhc (accessed November 10, 2020).

———. (2019b). "Preacher Perry Stone Checking His Phone," YouTube video, 01:41. Posted 27 September 2019. Retrieved from https://www.youtube.com/watch?v=3pw0fQfJUL0 (accessed 10 November 2020).

Palma, Sky (2019). "Preacher Stops to Check His Phone While Speaking in Tongues," *DeadState*, 28 September. Retrieved from https://deadstate.org/preacher-stops-to-check-his-phone-while-speaking-in-tongues/ (accessed 10 November 2020).

Perry Stone (2019). "Why I was looking at my phone...," YouTube video, 10:02. Posted 4 October 2019. Retrieved from https://www.youtube.com/watch?v=ETctmbBFs1o (accessed 10 November 2020).

Protestia (@Protestia) (2019). "Perry Stone Checks His Phone While 'Speaking in Tongues' (ICYMI) This would be pretty funny...if it weren't blasphemy of the Holy Spirit. https://t.co/I0iPTz5X0b." 2 November 2019, 6:05 PM. *Twitter*. Retrieved from https://twitter.com/Protestia/status/1190796987643432960?s=19 (accessed 10 November 2020).

Real Bible Believers (2019). "Satan Made Perry Stone Answer His Phone!!! | Dr. Gene Kim," YouTube video, 17:51. Posted 16 October 2019. Retrieved from https://www.youtube.com/watch?v=tpUEnV9phBM&fbclid=IwAR2is3Hi-r1FsfOho33LHMk1nxnZg1zoBfVgqimNqUuDNPyM41P2930dd2k (accessed 1 September 2020).

Schechner, Richard (2004). *Performance*. New York: Routledge.

Smith, Johnathan Z. (1987). *To Take Place: Toward Theory in Ritual*. Chicago: University of Chicago Press.

124 *Fabricating Authenticity*

Taru, Josiah (2019). "Mobile Apps and Religious Processes Among Pentacostal-Charismatic Christians in Zimbabwe." In Jacqueline H. Fewkes (ed.), *Anthropological Perspectives on the Religious Uses of Mobile Apps*, 153–173. Sham: Palgrave Macmillan. https://doi.org/10.1007/978-3-030-26376-8_8

21. Do People Misunderstand Their Own Religion?

Craig Martin

Is it possible for people to misunderstand their own religion or their own cultural tradition?

Some scholars appear to think so, such as Stephen Prothero in *Religious Literacy*, where he claims that Americans are really religious but don't understand their own religions. "Americans are both deeply religious and profoundly ignorant about religion. They are Protestants who can't name the four Gospels, Catholics who can't name the seven sacraments, and Jews who can't name the five books of Moses" (2008: 1).

On the one hand, if by this he means that "some people who identify as Christian don't know the history of all people throughout history who've similarly identified as Christian," or, "some people who identify as Christian don't know the contents of all of the texts that they hold, in name, to be sacred," who would object?

On the other, hand, I suspect that what he means is something along the lines of "Christians don't understand Christianity," which is a completely different proposition altogether.

Generally speaking, I've seen no empirical evidence that people are omniscient about themselves or the cultural traditions they inhabit, so I wouldn't allege that anyone comprehensively understands themselves or their tradition, but for the most part I would allege that people do tend to understand their own traditions. The problem is that, when talking about Christians, by "their own traditions" I don't mean "the history of all who've identified as Christians" or "the content of their nominal sacred texts." Rather, I think it is more useful

126   *Fabricating Authenticity*

to think of "their tradition" in terms of the local social practices they inhabit.

For example, the students at my college tend to identify as Catholic, but also tend to know very little about the history of Catholicism. When they say, "I'm Catholic," this usually appears to mean "my parents made me go to church, made me participate in a number of sacraments, and make me attend mass when I'm visiting them." Most of them know very little about the contents of the Bible, the history of the Catholic church, or the doctrines declared orthodox by the Vatican. In fact, every once in a while, a self-identified Catholic student is shocked (and disgusted) when I teach them the doctrine of transubstantiation.

Does this mean that they don't understand their own tradition? Not on my interpretation. Why? Because, if pressed, they understand very well the tenets, practices, and motivations of what is sometimes pejoratively called "nominal Catholicism." They report believing that they should be good or they'll go to hell, they know the bodily habits required by participation in mass, and they understand why they participate in the sacraments: because their family requires it, and will continue to require it if and when they get married—and if and when they have children, they'll be required to by their family to require their own children to participate as well.

I suspect that if we wrote Prothero or the Vatican and asked why participation in mass is necessary for Catholics, they would report back that it has something to do with the belief in the salvific power of Jesus' body and blood; it is doubtful that they would say participation in mass is necessary because one's parents said so.

However, the reason my students are participating in mass is likely not because they personally believe in or desire the salvific power of Jesus' body and blood; they're likely participating because their parents require it, and they know that's why they are participating. As such, these students likely understand the motivation behind their participation in mass better than Prothero or the officials of the institution. It wouldn't be fair to say that these students "don't understand Christianity." They might not understand Prothero's or the Vatican's version of Christianity, but they understand their own Christian practices quite well. In sum, there are many forms of Catholicism; the definition promulgated by the institution itself is only but one version.

The subtle aspects outlined in the case above matter as there are considerable political consequences to privileging an official institutional definition of a tradition over the one held by practitioners. Consider, for instance, Winnifred Fallers Sullivan's case study about Jewish and Catholic lay persons who filed a religious freedom lawsuit against the city of Boca Raton, Florida, because city officials took down the "religious" shrines they built over their loved ones' graves in a publicly owned cemetery (Sullivan 2005). The judge presiding over the case eventually ruled that there was no basis for their lawsuit, as their "religious" shrines weren't actually "religious," because they weren't required by the "religious" traditions they participated in. His judgment was based, in part, on the expert testimony of two religion scholars who provided a typology for interpreting their practices as insufficiently central to their religious traditions to count as religious.

Nathan Katz, for instance, distinguished between "High Traditions and Little Traditions":

> By "high tradition" is meant the textual-legal side of religion, usually male dominated and church or synagogue-centered. By "little tradition" is meant the folkways and home-centered observances, usually orally rather than textually transmitted, often the domain of women in a traditional culture. ... In contemporary America, the "little traditions" are often based in ethnicity, and one can make a distinction between practices which are "religious" and customs which are "ethnic," the "high" and the "low" traditions. (quoted in Sullivan 2005: 74)

For all practical purposes, what Katz is doing here is distinguishing the male-dominated, official institutional practices from the unofficial, female-led practices exercised outside of the institutional center. In doing so, he writes as if the dominant tradition did not itself reflect particular ethnic origins. This is not entirely different from one of the fantasies of whiteness: that "white" is "normal" rather than "ethnic," while non-white groups are "ethnic" and therefore "different from normal"—as if the dominant strand was universal rather than just another particular. Last, he designates the male-dominated tradition

128 *Fabricating Authenticity*

as "religious" and demotes the female-led, apparently ethnic traditions as "non-religious." Given that the plaintiffs make the case on the grounds of "religious freedom," the framework offered by Katz sets up religious freedom as something that extends first or primarily to men who are members of the dominant ethnic group who, as a result of male privilege and racial or ethnic dominance, are able to control institutions. The distribution of power and privilege could not be clearer: women and ethnic minorities don't get to define their "religion" because they don't control the institutions which Katz identifies as "high" rather than "little."

Similarly, Daniel Pals provided the judge in the case with a typology according to which authentic religion included practices that were authorized in sacred texts, ancient enough to be considered classic, and practiced across time and space within the tradition (Sullivan 2005: 79). The shrines produced by the plaintiffs in the case, Pals insisted, did not meet these criteria. "To the degree that Christians and Jews" built such shrines, "it is clear that they did so not as in any way a religious obligation, but as a matter of personal taste—and a preference rather strangely at odds with their own religious traditions" (quoted in Sullivan 2005: 81). He used the metaphor of a point with circling radii in to explain why these practices fell outside the center: "I find the metaphor of a circle or the image of a circle with, let us say, concentric rings or radii going out form the center to the edge the most useful for me to understand the nature of religious traditions" (ibid.: 81).

If Katz is right that the institutions at the center are typically monopolized by men who are members of the ethnic majority, apparently the practices of women and ethnic minorities fall under the periphery rather than the center. This would be consistent with Pals' claim that by "center" we make "the natural inference … we're talking about clergy and theologians and well established traditions on the one hand, which have protection, and the minor practices of lay folk, which do not" (ibid.: 82); it's clear that across the history of Christianity and Judaism, the center—at least as defined by Pals—has been populated and dominated by men and—at least since race and ethnicity have been invented—by men who are members of the dominant races or ethnicities.

The judge concurred with the claim that the "little," "lay," or "peripheral" practices exercised by the plaintiffs weren't sufficiently central to count as religious: "I would conclude from the expert witnesses that I heard ... that if I were to apply the test as I understand it under the Florida [religious freedom law], that this certainly, these views aren't central, they are not mandatory, and they are peripheral or marginal" (Sullivan 2005: 94). Consequently, he ruled that their shrines weren't protected by Florida's religious freedom laws.

By contrast with Katz and Pals, I would argue that these plaintiffs did not misunderstand their own cultural traditions; on the contrary, I would allege that what they counted as their tradition was just different from the versions promulgated by the Christian and Jewish elite institutions with which they partially identify.

Clearly, the definition of "tradition" was, in this court case, an act of power with political consequences. Who gets to define what is authentic tradition or religion, and what is not? Who benefits and who does not? Scholarly typologies are not politically neutral just because they are invented by scholars. Contrary to the approach taken by Katz and Pals, rather than define authentic tradition, I would argue that we as scholars should instead point to how people define their and others' traditions. Who identifies the tradition as what, in what context, and with what political consequences? Here, Katz, Pals, and the judge defined Judaism and Christianity in a way that excluded the practices of the plaintiffs, with the consequence that—given the judge's and the scholars' institutional authority—the plaintiffs' desires were thwarted. By contrast, the plaintiffs defined their practices as Jewish and Christian practices, but in a context wherein they lacked authority, such that they were insufficiently persuasive to the political powers to win the protections they desired.

On the approach I'm advocating, we needn't commit to Prothero's view that anyone misunderstands their own tradition, a claim that in some cases has real political consequences. One benefit, in my opinion, is that we as scholars are less likely to be pawns in political contests as a result of this self-limitation.

130   *Fabricating Authenticity*

Craig Martin, Ph.D., is Professor of Religious Studies at St. Thomas Aquinas College. He writes on poststructuralism, discourse analysis, and ideology critique; his most recent books include *Discourse and Ideology: A Critique of the Study of Culture* (Bloomsbury Academic, 2022) and *A Critical Introduction to the Study of Religion, Third Edition* (Routledge, 2023).

References

Prothero, Stephen (2008). *Religious Literacy: What Every American Needs to Know—And Doesn't.* New York, NY: HarperCollins.

Sullivan, Winnifred Fallers (2005). *The Impossibility of Religious Freedom.* Princeton, NJ: Princeton University Press.

22. But Is It Really Religion?

Savannah H. Finver

How do we know which groups count as *real* religions, and who gets to decide?

The status of Pastafarianism as a religion in the United States has recently been up for debate. Pastafarians are perhaps best known for the colanders they wear on their heads, though they are also sometimes pictured wearing traditional pirate garb. The Flying Spaghetti Monster, depicted as a blob of spaghetti noodles with two meatballs in its body and two eye stalks, serves as their god, and their organization, mostly consisting of online membership, is called the Church of the Flying Spaghetti Monster. According to their webpage, they have existed in secret for "hundreds of years," but only came to the public's attention around 2006 when the group's figurehead, Bobby Henderson, wrote an open letter to the Kansas School Board requesting that the Church's creation story be taught in public schools as an alternative theory of Intelligent Design (Henderson 2006). The theory of Intelligent Design postulates that the universe is so immensely complex that it must have been built intentionally by an intelligent creator, most typically the so-called Judeo-Christian god. In his letter, which can also be found on the group's webpage, Henderson alleges that there is no more proof that the Judeo-Christian god is the Designer behind the universe than the Flying Spaghetti Monster. Since the United States Constitution forbids the states from taking an official position in favor of any particular religion, Henderson insists that any discussion of an intelligent designer taking place in a public school must make mention of the Flying Spaghetti Monster (ibid.).

Perhaps it feels natural to laugh when one sees pictures of people wearing colanders on their heads, people dressed in what appear to be pirate costumes, or illustrations depicting the Flying Spaghetti

132 *Fabricating Authenticity*

Monster (FSM). The Church of the FSM has been widely described by the public, by scholars, and in legal discourse as a parody of "real" religion. In the United States, the Church of the FSM still has not been legally designated as a "church" per the qualifications set forth by the Internal Revenue Service (IRS). One case, *Cavanaugh v. Bartelt* (2016), in which the plaintiff sued prison officials for allegedly refusing to accommodate his religious requests, advanced to the District Court of Nebraska before a judge dismissed it, writing,

> The Court finds that FSMism is not a "religion" within the meaning of the relevant federal statutes and constitutional jurisprudence. It is, rather, a parody, intended to advance an argument about science, the evolution of life, and the place of religion in public education. Those are important issues, and FSMism contains a serious argument—but that does not mean that the trappings of the satire used to make that argument are entitled to protection as a "religion." (ibid.)

Asma T. Uddin, lawyer and outspoken defender of religious freedom protections, writes about *Cavanaugh* in her recent book, *When Islam is Not a Religion* (2019), in which she suggests that cases about groups such as Pastafarianism "are the easier cases" for judges to decide since they contain "claims of religion" which are "an obvious ruse" (2019: 125). Joseph P. Laycock, a religious studies scholar, recently wrote the first full-length monograph exploring The Satanic Temple (TST), a group of Satanists who, Laycock explains in his introduction, are often painted by the media as a political stunt or a hoax. Though Laycock criticizes TST's critics for missing the way in which TST can help us rethink how the boundaries between religion and politics are policed, he unironically refers to Pastafarians only a few pages later as "a satirical 'parody' religion," even though both groups have engaged in similar political activities (2020: 6).

That the general public, the legal system, and especially scholars seem to have no trouble jumping to the conclusion that Pastafarianism simply can't be a real or serious religion, despite the group's claims to the contrary, speaks to the central questions posed in Craig Martin's chapter. He asks us, as scholars and critical thinkers, to consider "[w]ho gets to define what is authentic tradition or religion, and what

FINVER *But Is It Really Religion?* 133

is not? Who benefits and who does not?" (Chapter 21). It seems clear, based on the claims made on the Church of FSM's webpage, that Pastafarians themselves identify their group as a real religion. At the bottom of the "About" page, in the "Questions and Answers" section, the stated response to the question "Is this a joke?" reads:

> It's not a joke. Elements of our religion are sometimes described as satire and there are many members who do not literally believe our scripture, but this isn't unusual in religion. A lot of Christians don't believe the Bible is literally true—but that doesn't mean they aren't True Christians. ("About" n.d.)

The Church of FSM's response to this question refers to a similar point Martin makes in his opening example, where he describes how many of his students who identify as Catholic "know very little about the contents of the Bible, the history of the Catholic church, or the doctrines declared orthodox by the Vatican" (Chapter 21). For Martin, this doesn't indicate that his students aren't *real* Catholics; it simply means that what counts as Catholicism for them may be somewhat different than what others, including institutional authorities, would describe as "real" or "official" Catholicism. In fact, for Martin, even taking part in such discussions about what counts as "real" Catholicism implicates scholars in a political conversation about which behaviors deserve social and legal legitimation and which do not.

I would extend Martin's critique even further and contend that when scholars describe some groups as "religions" and others as parody, satire, or hoaxes, they engage in a similar political move whereby some groups are implicitly authenticated and others are delegitimized. Martin writes that "[s]cholarly typologies are not politically neutral just because they are invented by scholars" (Chapter 21). In other words, if we engage in discussions about what counts as "real" religion, we implicate ourselves—especially in the United States—in a legal question regarding which groups are deserving of special rights, protections, and exemptions from the government. Rather than involve ourselves in such authenticity claims, we may find it more useful to explore what creates such a strong social consensus that groups like the Pastafarians *shouldn't* count as real religion, why

134 *Fabricating Authenticity*

other groups (such as Christianity, Judaism, or Islam) are seemingly automatically granted the status of real religions today, and what rights and privileges are distributed and withheld as a result of these discussions.

Savannah H. Finver is a doctoral student at Ohio State University where she is pursuing a degree in Comparative Studies. Her interests lie in discourses on religion as they appear in U.S. law and politics, especially as they pertain to the assignment of civil rights and legal privileges.

References

"About" (n.d.). *The Church of the Flying Spaghetti Monster*. Retrieved from https://www.spaghettimonster.org/about/.

Cavanaugh v. Bartelt (2016). 178 F. Supp. 3d 819 (D. Neb. 2016).

Henderson, Bobby (2006). "Open Letter to the Kansas School Board." *The Church of the Flying Spaghetti Monster*. Retrieved from https://www.spaghettimonster.org/pages/about/open-letter/.

Laycock, Joseph P. (2020). *Speak of the Devil: How the Satanic Temple Is Changing the Way We Talk About Religion*. New York, NY: Oxford University Press.

Uddin, Asma T. (2019). *When Islam is Not a Religion: Inside America's Fight for Religious Freedom*. New York, NY: Pegasus Books, Ltd.

23. If It's Not Authentic, It's Not a Religion

Teemu Taira

On 16 December 2016, the Charity Commission (CC) of England and Wales announced that the Temple of the Jedi Order does not satisfy the required criteria for being registered as a charity on the basis of advancement of religion. The government website where the decision file is hosted explains, "This is a significant decision because the commission had to consider the definition of religion in charity law" (Decision 2016).

Depending on the law and country, there are many criteria used in such decision-making, but "authenticity" is rarely one of them. For instance, this word is not found in the CC decision concerning the Temple of the Jedi Order (TOTJO). In most cases, however, the idea of "authenticity" haunts the process. People wonder whether this or that qualifies as a real or authentic religion, and there are several aspects which may lead them to conclude that the criteria for authenticity are not met—even when no one has clarified what authenticity refers to. Although "authenticity" is a term used elsewhere in public discourse, in legal contexts authenticity typically operates as an unspoken meta-category that unifies explicitly mentioned criteria in thinking about religion. In order to have a religion, one has to fabricate an aura of authenticity in addition to fulfilling the explicit criteria mentioned in the law. In other words, meeting the explicit criteria is not enough—and those are often relatively vague and open for interpretation. One also has to convince others that the religion is not a scam, fraud, joke or otherwise "inauthentic."

According to the charity law, "religion" requires belief, worship, moral value and "a certain level of cogency, seriousness, cohesion

136 *Fabricating Authenticity*

and importance" (Decision 2016: 3). The CC declared that Jediism is not characterized by a belief in gods or other spiritual or non-secular entities. It did not find enough evidence of worship that expressed a relationship between the adherents and the object of belief. Despite agreeing that Jediism upholds specific, potentially beneficial values, it did not find "sufficient evidence to conclude that TOTJO promotes doctrines and practice of benefit to the public" (ibid.: 6). As for the last criterion, the Commission stated that it "considers that there is insufficient evidence that Jediism ... is a sufficiently structured, organised or integrated system of belief to constitute a religion" (ibid.).

Given the vagueness of definitions in law, none of the four criteria can be formally examined without taking into consideration the cultural impact of what constitutes real or authentic religion for people. But the last one—cogency, seriousness, cohesion, and importance—is particularly open for cultural interpretation. So here comes a guide for fabricating an authentic religion that may be taken as cogent and serious, after fulfilling the other criteria used for determining whether a group counts as religious.

To start, it should not be considered a joke or parody. This has been a problem with Pastafarianism and, to a lesser extent, Jediism. However, "not being taken as a joke" is not sufficient to be taken seriously. One should be able to present the group as unified and homogeneous, rather than diverse. One should claim that there are centralized authority structures; if some adherents think differently, they should be labeled as inauthentic heretics. One should not give an impression that the belief system is a loose framework of ideas where adherents have space for subjective evaluation. Thus, it is not a path where individuals explore their inner selves subjectively but a collective one where doctrines are clear, fixed and handed down by leading authorities to the adherents. One should not state that some adherents may not want to call it a religion; by calling it a philosophy, worldview, or a way of life, they are misrepresenting the authentic essence of a religion. Moreover, one should be clear that this is an exclusive religion that one cannot mix eclectically with other belief systems. One should also be willing to use such words as spiritual, sacred, ritual, and worship extensively, even when one is not sure what they actually refer to (see Owen and Taira 2015).

One further strategy in fabricating authentic religion is to imagine the past as a more or less uninterrupted tradition. When *Karhun kansa* (People of the Bear) applied for the status of a registered religious community in Finland, they claimed to follow pre-Christian Finnish religion. The committee did not believe that to be possible, due to a lack of sources. In response, the group admitted that they cannot claim to perform a fully authentic reconstruction of the religion, but they attempt to follow the spirit of the ancient Finnish beliefs and rituals. That worked.

But what happens when there is nothing else than the recent past? The origin narrative of Jediism goes no further back in time than the 1977 film *Star Wars*. One possible solution is to suggest that the truths of Jediism are eternal and that the film simply discovered them. This strategy may work only if the time of discovery is far enough back in history. Furthermore, previous models that meet the expectations are needed; otherwise, the fabrication is deemed inauthentic. Therefore, "religions" claiming to build on the basis of an existing "world religion" have a much better chance to be taken seriously than others. One example is Diamond Way Buddhism, founded by a Danish couple five years before the first *Star Wars* movie. It has been successful in being classified as a religious group, primarily because it was branded as a form of Buddhism.

It is by such means that one might be able to convince others of authenticity, though I do not claim that the list is exhaustive. Perhaps the most interesting point is not to figure out how Jediism or similar groups may succeed in presenting themselves as authentic religions, but in thinking what sort of authenticity has been fabricated by negotiating and denying the validity of Jediism in the context of religion.

Why does the authenticity of Jediism matter at all? Why not let all the flowers bloom? What is the harm in Jediism having charitable status? It is to be noted that authenticity is a contrastive term. It is used in demarcating one's preferred entity from an "inauthentic" one. It is also something that people want. Moreover, if something is conceived as authentic, it deserves veneration and admiration (Potter 2010). If Jediism were to be granted charitable status on the basis of advancement of religion, it would be a substantial step toward the legitimation of Jediism as a religion in general (although in a narrow

138 *Fabricating Authenticity*

technical sense it would be simply a decision limited to charitable status).

Not completely unlike Walter Benjamin's (1973) idea of the aura of a work of art, the fabrication of the aura of authenticity protects the category of religion by making "religion" something special and unique. Although it would be possible to suggest in theory that religion is a blurred and invented category that is used for the sake of convenience in charity law to distribute privileges to groups that do something good for the whole of society, in practice this would be inconceivable. This is because it would strip the aura of authenticity from "religion" in general. Who, then, benefits from the fact that the category of religion is in operation in society where an "inauthentic" religion does not count as religion at all? In addition to selected minority groups, perhaps it is beneficial for the continuation of Christian hegemony—which in many ways is shaking, if not disappearing—because there has probably never been a fully established discourse on religion without Christianity at its center.

Teemu Taira is Senior Lecturer in the Study of Religion, University of Helsinki. His research interests focus on the category of "religion" in public discourse, religion in the media, and atheist identifications. His recent publications include *Taking "Religion" Seriously: Essays on the Discursive Study of Religion* (Brill, 2022) and *Atheism in Five Minutes* (Equinox Publishing Ltd., 2022). For more information, see: teemutaira.wordpress.com.

References

Benjamin, Walter (1973). *Illuminations*. London: Fontana Press.

Decision (2016). Decision: The Temple of the Jedi Order. *Gov.uk*. https://www.gov.uk/government/publications/the-temple-of-the-jedi-order

Owen, Suzanne, and Teemu Taira (2015). "The Category of 'Religion' in Public Classification: Charity Registration of the Druid Network in England and Wales." In Trevor Stack, Naomi R. Goldenberg, and Timothy Fitzgerald (eds.), *Religion as a Category of Governance and Sovereignty*, 90–114. Leiden: Brill. https://doi.org/10.1163/9789004290594_006

Potter, Andrew (2010). *The Authenticity Hoax: How We Get Lost Finding Ourselves*. New York: HarperCollins.

24. Rebranding Religion: Authenticity, Representation, and the Marketplace

Zabeen Khamisa

What is "good" religion, what makes it *authentic*, and according to whom? What allows for religions to be classified as either "good" or "bad" and what is at stake in this classification? In Teemu Taira's analysis of the Jedi Temple Order and the manufacturing of Jediism, he outlines how some social groups are determined as authentic religions because they fit within the legal parameters of what constitutes "religion" as determined by law. In Taira's discussion, he also outlines how the legal authenticity of a religion is determined by a social groups' ability to prove its benefit to society, while maintaining a proximity to prescribed religion as determined by charity law, thus drawing a correlation between the social economy, "good" religion, and authenticity. Taira's example demonstrates how bureaucratic institutions in public life (of any country really)—whether law, education, health care, art, etc.—play a concrete role in the classification of authentic religion. However, as Taira points out, institutions like law in the UK—not unlike that of Canada and America— prioritize certain conceptions of religion that implicitly (if not explicitly) equate religion with Christian hegemony. So, what happens when non-Christian groups not only fall outside of "good" or "authentic" religion like the Jedi Temple Order, but also are explicitly classified as "bad" religion? How do religious adherents uphold and/or challenge the fabrication of these classifications?

Consider the post-9/11 political climate for Muslims and Sikhs in America. For example, narratives of "good" Muslims (liberal, western, secular values) and "bad" Muslims (radical extremists

140   *Fabricating Authenticity*

and terrorists) were perpetuated by the evolving Islamophobia industry—fears which were informed by the pervasive, structural assumptions about religion as understood through Christian hegemony, American political ideologies, and Western democracy and economics (Mamdani 2005). Visible Muslims (those who wear head coverings like hijabs, for example) were targets of racism and xenophobia. Perhaps less known are the ways Sikhs, especially turbaned and bearded Sikhs, were also targeted in this context. In these cases, Sikhs were mistaken as Muslims based on their resembling appearance (Luthra 2018).

To counter the violence and discrimination following 9/11, many Muslims and Sikhs felt inclined to create public educational campaigns, as well as charitable organizations, to dispel the notion that all Muslims and Sikhs are terrorists, to demonstrate that they too condemn terrorism, and to emphasize their brand of "good" Islam or "good" Sikhi as authentic, (whether intentional or not) distancing themselves from politically radicalized groups. Such legitimizing practices have utilized the socio-economic domain. For example, the U.S.-based nonprofit National Sikh Campaign launched a one-million-dollar public awareness advertising campaign called "We are Sikhs" as an effort to educate Americans of the Sikh religion ("About" n.d.). The campaign included television advertisements during prominent sports games, a website, as well as a comprehensive social media outreach program. The ads feature Sikhs enthusiastically describing how their religious values align with American values. By drawing on their understandings of American ideologies, some Muslims and Sikhs in North America have understood the benefits of claiming alignment with hegemonic societal norms to better position themselves within a political framework as abiding citizens to prevent further discrimination, attempting to bring about systemic change.

Of course, these adaptive strategies rooted in the politics of representation and recognition were not met without critique. In my own fieldwork, I encountered Sikh progressive activists who saw this appeal to Americanness as the enabling of oppressive structures like capitalism, colonialism, and pandering to a neoliberal agenda, contributing to the further marginalization of their communities. Such a response demonstrates that there can be competing notions of "good" religion. Without a doubt, the privileges of the hegemonic paradigm play out in economic terms via the capitalist system that is reinforced by the free market principle. In this context, it is hard not to see the competing claims of authenticity in the branding of market goods in the name of diversity.

The competitive paradigm of good religion and bad religion runs parallel to good brands and bad brands when considering growing concerns around corporate social responsibility, ethical consumption, and cultural appropriation. Here, I want to bring to attention the discourse about authentic religion and representation in the free market. While there has been an increase in representation of marginalized communities in marketing campaigns, some Sikhs have noted the lack of self-representation in media forms, particularly of those Sikhs who don the turban. Despite this feeling of marginalization, several clothing manufacturers have used Sikh turbans in their clothing lines, without credit given to Sikhs, and excluding Sikh models and Sikh fashion designers. The most recent case was when Nordstrom included a Gucci-designed turban in their collection and tried to sell it for over $700. Sikh fashion entrepreneurs and activists called out Nordstrom for cultural appropriation and the product was removed from the line. In doing so, Sikh fashion social entrepreneurs and activists made claims that turbans—and the authentic Khalsa identity—should be designed and determined by Sikhs themselves, for authenticity and respect of their own religious practices. In addition, they suggested that turbans should not be costly items, so as to remain accessible to the people, reflective of the Sikh value of equity.

In my research about millennial Sikhs and as I've discussed elsewhere (Khamisa 2020), young entrepreneurial Sikh activists have responded to such fashion conundrums by creating Sikh fashion social enterprises. For some Sikhs the social economy becomes one avenue in which religious adherents have attempted to legitimize their authenticity. Separating from the for-profit enterprises, their work is more closely aligned with non-profits, or social enterprises—with a bottom-line that prioritizes addressing society's most complex problems such as, but not limited to, gender inequity and environmental degradation, and any profits are reinvested in the mission. One example of a Sikh-based and run social enterprise is The Trendy Singh

142 *Fabricating Authenticity*

(@TheTrendySingh, and sometimes referred to as TrendySingh), and it focuses on gender equality by creating printed floral turbans for all genders, the proceeds of which are invested in Sikh philanthropic organizations. The models and designers of The Trendy Singh are also Sikh. The Trendy Singh outlines its mission by articulating the Sikh values of social equity, charitable giving, and volunteerism (Comber 2018). Self-representation and these "good" values rooted in the Sikh tradition function to legitimize the activities of the entrepreneurs. At the same time, providing young Sikhs turbans with hip patterns to wear is supposed to help them feel more comfortable and cool and to disarm threatening on-lookers.

As noted by Teemu Taira in the previous chapter, often the policy definitions of religion determined by official national institutions in America and Canada are limited and reproduce or further the Christian hegemonic paradigm. While institutional definitions of religion attempt to posit a standard of what is considered religion, or right or good religion, often these parameters are at odds with the diversity and lived realities as experienced by religious adherents in their day-to-day lives. In the study of religion, the turn to lived religions was an attempt to decenter institutional definitions of religion and to problematize the stronghold of institutional authorities over the often-competing authenticities within a community by recognizing that these traditions are not monoliths. Those who require fewer accommodations, whose religion exists in proximity to official institutional definitions of religion, or secularism, get away with being good enough, or good religion, because they're seemingly less fussy. However, those marginalized non-Christian religious communities that seek out accommodations and advocate for institutional changes to these definitions are required to make the argument that their religion is also good religion and that their needs are authentic to their goodness to benefit from these institutions. In this sense they must find other ways to legitimize their group. Thus, I'm not interested in prescribing how religious groups ought to legitimize their authenticity. As a scholar of religion, I'm interested in the claims of authenticity and how religious practitioners conceive, adapt, and create processes of legitimacy.

Zabeen Khamisa is a doctoral candidate in the joint Wilfrid Laurier University-University of Waterloo Ph.D. program, Religious Diversity in North America. Zabeen's research interests include the study of religion, socio-political movements, Sikhi in North America, digital media and technology, and cultural economics. Her dissertation research is focused on progressive Sikh millennials in Canada.

References

"About" (n.d.). *We Are Sikhs*. Retrieved from https://www.wearesikhs.org/about.

Comber, Sarah (2018). "Trendy Singh is Breaking Barriers Through Creating Wearable Art." *Vern Magazine*, 18 January. Retrieved from https://www.vernmagazine.com/trendy-singh-breaking-barriers-creating-wearable-art/.

Khamisa, Zabeen (2020). "Disruptive Garb: Gender Production and Millennial Sikh Fashion Enterprises in Canada," *Religions* 11/4: 160. https://doi.org/10.3390/rel11040160

Luthra, Sangeeta (2018). "Sikh American Millennials at Work: Institution Building, Activism, and a Renaissance of Cultural Expression." *Sikh Formations* 14/3–4: 280–299. https://doi.org/10.1080/17448727.2018.1485374

Mamdani, Mahmood (2005). *Good Muslim, Bad Muslim: America, the Cold War, and the Roots of Terror*. New York: Three Leaves Press.

25. Is There Neo-Nazi DNA?: Ancestry Tests and Biological Essentialism in American Racism

Martha Smith

The vision of white racial purity that drove the Nazi regime to perpetrate genocide in the mid-twentieth century has persisted into the present, most recently made visible by American white supremacist groups. The idea that bodies not only represented but also manifested an essential cultural supremacy may seem to be an outdated and backward view of the world. And yet, a recent surge in popular interest in ancestry and DNA may reveal the ways in which biological essentialism continues to inform popular American notions of identity.

In the wake of the 2017 Ku Klux Klan (KKK) rally in Charlottesville, VA, articles and exposés on the alt-right, KKK, white supremacy, and neo-Nazi movements in America were flooding newsfeeds everywhere. Two of those recent articles connect white nationalist movements with ancestry and DNA testing, raising questions about our general assumptions on relationship between biology and identity. Headlines, such as Sarah Zhang's article in *The Atlantic*, "When White Nationalists Get DNA Tests That Reveal African Ancestry" (Zhang 2017), and Tom Hale's post on IFLScience, "White Supremacists Taking Ancestry Tests Aren't Happy About The Results" (Hale 2017) play on the generally assumed biological basis of identity.

These headlines work on multiple levels, but mainly by assuming that the reader will automatically guess the irony of white supremacists having non-white ancestry. This notion itself reveals a lot about our own categories of identity—if white supremacists discovering they are not "really" white is the point of these exercises, we are assuming that ancestry tests will confound white supremacist's own categories of biological essentialism (remember those "blood and soil" chanters in Virginia?; Wagner 2017). However, a closer reading of these articles reveals the ways in which even the staunchest believers in biological descent as the foundation of identity can easily transform meaning when those categories are challenged. At the same time, opponents of white supremacists also maintain certain assumptions about biological ancestry and identity.

Many of these articles cite the recent research by sociologists Aaron Panofsky and Joan Donovan, who studied the ways in which members of Stormfront (a white supremacist forum) responded to genetic ancestry tests (GATs). What they found was an overwhelming tendency of white supremacists to interpret the tests in ways that simply reimagine and reconstitute white identity. That is, even if their ancestry did not reveal a genetic "purity," they remained confident in their purity by simply reinterpreting their results to fit their existing categories. As Panofsky and Donovan note, "Despite their essentialist views of race, much less than using the information to police individuals' membership, posters expend considerable energy to repair identities by rejecting or reinterpreting GAT results" (2017: 1). But should we be surprised by these findings? Perhaps, but only if we expect genetic ancestry tests to have some connection to biological identity *outside* of interpretive categories. This leads to a bigger question: When do we deploy the rhetoric of biological essentialism? And to what ends?

Maybe you have seen ancestry test commercials that feature individuals whose results make them challenge who they are at a deeper level (AncestryDNA 2017a; momondo 2016). In these instances, ancestry is advertised as a way to connect to others through the recognition of one's own genetic profile, which is never as clear-cut as the participants assume (see also McCutcheon 2016). The DNA Discussion Project is one example of a university program that encourages their community to "talk about diversity in a new, positive and engaging way" by providing "ancestry DNA tests to hundreds of students, faculty, and staff at the University" in order "to help them find out who they *really* are" (2006; emphasis added). While

146 *Fabricating Authenticity*

this may work for those who are looking to reinforce multicultural identities or find new facets of "who they really are" (Donnella 2017), it also points to the ways in which race and ethnicity remain tied to biology even for those who want to use these categories to undermine racism. In fact, we should note that these more progressive ends can also go awry. A good example of the appropriation made possible by ancestry tests can be found in stories about the "uncovering" of Native American identity (for example, see AncestryDNA 2017b; Crossan 2016). In these cases, genetic testing allows white Americans to claim Indigenous identity even if they have no lived experience with Indigenous communities. Genetic testing may provide evidence of shared ancestry, but that does not always result in acceptance into communities bounded by racial or ethnic categories. Nor does it necessarily promote pluralism in the ways that participants hope it will. These examples illustrate the competing claims around what constitutes "authentic" identity. Is one Native American because of ancestry or experience? Or is it always much more complicated than these simple distinctions imply? Using ancestry tests to confirm an embodied, core identity ignores the many other ways humans constitute ethnic and racial identity. Advertisements for GATs often claim that they provide a clear, genetic answer to questions of identity; however, the results are subject to multiple interpretative frameworks with competing claims around authenticity.

Should we be surprised that GATs can be deployed to achieve so many different ends? Ancestry tests may seem to have two simple interpretive outcomes: in the most generous reading they allow individuals to connect to identities previously seen as foreign or other, in the worst-case scenario they contribute to ideologies of racial purity like those at work in the Nazi final solution. However, both of these interpretations rely on biological essentialism to inform identity construction. In this light, genetic ancestry tests reveal much more about our social constructions of reality than they do about any "really real" identity waiting to be uncovered. In fact, it is around the new and unpredictable *interpretive* possibilities of genetic research that many scholars have very real concerns about the future of biological essentialism and American racism. Sarah Zhang sums this up well in her *Atlantic* article, quoted below. And while white supremacists' interpretations of genetic testing are overtly racist, the widespread use of ancestry tests by ordinary people looking to find authenticity in their genetic codes reminds us that biological essentialism remains a powerful marker of identity for many Americans.

> The problem is not with the science per se, but with the set of underlying assumptions about race that we always imprint on the latest science. True, genetics has led to real breakthroughs in medicine, but it is also the latest in a centuries-long effort to understand biological differences. "In a sense, genetics is a modern version of what early scientists were doing in terms of their studies of skulls or blood type," says Ann Morning, a sociologist at New York University. "We have a long history of turning to whatever we think is the most authoritative sense of knowledge and expecting to find race proved or demonstrated there." And like its predecessors, genetics is vulnerable to misuse by those with racist agendas (Zhang 2016).

Martha Smith is Professor of Religious Studies at Fullerton College in Southern California. Her current research and teaching interests include North American religious diversity and pluralism, race and ethnicity studies, diversity and social justice. Her courses focus on the diversity of the American religious landscape, especially the ways in which race, gender, and ethnicity are connected to religious identities and the significance of material culture and lived religious experience in American life.

References

AncestryDNA (2017a). "Livie: Father's Day," iSpot.tv video, 00:28. Posted 7 June 2017 (2 September 2016). Retrieved from https://www.ispot.tv/ad/wDMp/ancestrydna-testimonial-livie.

———. (2017b). "Kim," iSpot.tv video, 00:28. Posted 17 Sept. 2017 (28 July 2016). Retrieved from https://ispot.tv/ad/wKqV/ancestrydna-kim.

Crossan, Andrea (2016). "You Took a DNA Test and It Says You Are Native American. So What?" *Public Radio International*, 24 November. Retrieved from https://www.pri.org/stories/2016-11-24/you-took-dna-test-and-it-says-you-are-native-american-so-what (accessed 21 January 2020).

148 *Fabricating Authenticity*

"DNA Discussion Project" (2006). *West Chester University*. Retrieved from https://www.wcupa.edu/DNADiscussion/ (accessed 21 January 2020).

Donnella, Leah (2017). "When 'Where Are You From?' Takes You Someplace Unexpected," *NPR*, 10 August. Retrieved from https://www.npr.org/sections/codeswitch/2017/08/10/541921634/when-where-are-you-from-takes-you-someplace-unexpected (accessed 21 January 2020).

Hale, Tom (2017). "White Supremacists Taking Ancestry Tests Aren't Happy About The Results," *IFLScience*, 17 August. Retrieved from https://www.iflscience.com/plants-and-animals/white-supremacists-taking-ancestry-tests-arent-happy-about-the-results/ (accessed 21 January 2020).

McCutcheon, Russell T. (2016). "Clash of Classifications," *Culture on the Edge: A Peer Reviewed Blog* (blog), 3 June. Retrieved from https://edge.ua.edu/russell-mccutcheon/clash-of-classifications/ (accessed 21 January 2020).

momondo (2016). "momondo—The DNA Journey," YouTube video, 05:16. Posted 2 June 2016. Retrieved from https://www.youtube.com/watch?v=tyaEQEmt5ls.

Panofsky, Aaron, and Joan Donovan (2017). "Genetic Ancestry Testing among White Nationalists." *SocArXiv*, 17 August. https://doi.org/10.31235/osf.io/7f9bc (accessed 21 January 2020).

Wagner, Meg. (2017). "'Blood and Soil': Protesters Chant Nazi Slogan in Charlottesville," *CNN*, 12 August. Retrieved from https://www.cnn.com/2017/08/12/us/charlottesville-unite-the-right-rally/index.html (accessed 21 January 2020).

Zhang, Sarah (2016). "Will the Alt-Right Peddle a New Kind of Racist Genetics?" *The Atlantic*, 29 December. Retrieved from https://www.theatlantic.com/science/archive/2016/12/genetics-race-ancestry-tests/510962/ (accessed 21 January 2020).

———. (2017). "When White Nationalists Get DNA Tests That Reveal African Ancestry." *The Atlantic*, 17 August. Retrieved from https://www.theatlantic.com/science/archive/2017/08/white-nationalists-dna-ancestry/537108/ (accessed 21 January 2020).

26. Making Sense of a Sense of Self

Israel L. Domínguez

I would like to begin by acknowledging the lands on which Gloria and I were both raised—what is now frequently called the Rio Grande Valley of Texas—is the occupied, unceded land of the Coahuiltecan and Carrizo peoples.

In the interest of self-positionality, I am a queer, brown, Chicano, Tejano millennial whose research focuses on healing and decolonizing along the U.S.-Mexico border. My research is absolutely dependent on the work of Gloria Anzaldúa. A queer Latina theorist, activist, poet, and author born and raised in the Rio Grande Valley of south Texas, Anzaldúa is known for her works on Chicana feminist and queer theories. Her book *Borderlands/La Frontera: The New Mestiza* (1987) uses highly evocative, sensual language to grapple with decolonizing, particularly by empowering Indigeneity and addressing alternative sexualities. She stresses the importance of actively using one's Indigeneity to their advantage—not as something to be ashamed of, but as something from which to draw strength. Anzaldúa very briefly introduces her theory of nepantla in this book when examining the intersections of Indigeneity and alternatively gendered and/or sexually oriented.

A Nahuatl word, nepantla roughly translates to "in-between space." Nahuatl is an Indigenous Uto-Aztecan language spoken throughout northern and central Mexico; pronounced "NA-watl," the frequently-appearing tl phoneme represents a single sound and should not be separated. Anzaldúa describes nepantla as a place where one can work through issues of identity in ways which are productive and generative, despite societal demands and traditions.

150 *Fabricating Authenticity*

In her posthumous work *Light in the Dark* (2015), Anzaldúa writes: "Nepantla is the place where my cultural and personal codes clash, where I come up against the world's dictates ... Nepantla is the point of contact y el lugar between worlds—between imagination and physical existence, between ordinary and nonordinary (spirit) realities" (2015: 2). She subsequently extends this personal, intimate tension to society at large and claims the ongoing navigation of this in-between space—this liminality between cultural and social boundaries—is where change can be reached. "In nepantla we undergo the anguish of changing our perspectives and crossing a series of cruz calles, junctures, and thresholds, some leading to a different way of relating to people and surroundings and others to the creation of a new world" (ibid.: 17).

I am forefronting my response to Martha Smith's chapter with this explanation of Anzaldúa because it was resounding through my mind as I read about genetic ancestry tests (GATs) and their various uses and implications. Due to the effects of European colonization of the Américas, genetic ancestry can be something particularly pertinent to a Latinx person in poignant ways. The colonial matrix of power works in part by systemizing the erasure of Indigenous facets of society and culture, and so, it is exceedingly common to find people of Latinx descent across the American hemisphere who are not able to cite or trace their Indigenous heritages at all (Quijano and Ennis 2000). My father, for example, was able to find a distant cousin who had done genealogical work for their visibly-mestizo (that is, interracial heritage particularly pertaining to indigenous and Iberian descent) family, identifying various branches of Spanish ancestors—spanning centuries—and connecting them to original homes in Asturias and Aragón. However, there was absolutely no information recorded about Native American branches, even though most of my father's relatives (himself, included) clearly possessed phenotypical markers often associated with Indigenous heritage. His story is not an unusual one. The gaps in his family tree often teased me as I grew older, and so, when cost-effective GATs became publicly available, I jumped at the chance to have us both try one out and see what information could be gleaned. I considered the opportunity an avenue

DOMÍNGUEZ *Making Sense of a Sense of Self* 151

for illuminating a potential heritage elided at best and erased at worst by the brutalization of colonization.

Pivoting toward a gesture made in Smith's piece, I would like to expand on her analysis a bit more explicitly. As someone who grew up in an area of the nation described as a "shock culture, a border culture, a third country, a closed country," and "una herida abierta where the Third World grates against the first and bleeds" (Anzaldúa 1987: 3, 11), I have frequently had to grapple with issues of cultural appropriation and cultural insensitivity. From non-Latinx, white friends wearing a sombrero "as a joke;" to well-meaning, non-Latinx, white women "teaching" me Mexico is actually diverse; to public school educators telling me I surely cannot be full Mexican since I looked "too clean," I have wondered why some people feel they have the authority to speak on issues which, at least at first glance, do not seem to concern them. It wasn't until I entered the academy that I gained the ability to verbalize my discomforts; namely, how sometimes there is a difference between one's culture and one's heritage, and often, there are many who do not reckon with that. I see echoes of this specifically in Smith's piece when she discusses how white supremacists "simply reimagine and reconstitute white identity" (Chapter 25).

Smith writes how "a recent surge in popular interest in ancestry and DNA may reveal the ways in which biological essentialism continues to inform popular American notions of identity" (Chapter 25), which certainly was the case for my father and my teenage self, though for us specifically, it was less a search for authenticity or an authentic self, and more a search for … well, anything—any kind of information which could fill in the blanks. We certainly were not looking for "who we really were," and looking back, I am not entirely sure if I could specify what we were looking for exactly. There was just so little information at all, any scrap would have been fantastic. My father has passed, but I still take lessons from our endeavor, especially as a scholar of the effects and processes of colonization in the U.S.-Mexico borderlands. It has not been a search for an essence or an essentialized, reductive self. For me personally, it has been a chance simply to look at the past and my present through different lenses, lenses which allow me to pierce through the fog of colonization and

152 *Fabricating Authenticity*

perchance catch a glimpse of a forgotten name or practice or locale—anything which can break up the illusion of an all-white past. This leads me back to Anzaldúa and nepantla:

> Nepantla is the site of transformation, the place where different perspectives come into conflict and where you question the basic ideas, tenets, and identities inherited from your family, your education, and your different cultures. Nepantla is the zone between changes where you struggle to find equilibrium between the outer expression of change and your inner relationship to it. ... *From the in-between place of nepantla, you see through the fiction of the monoculture.* (2015: 127; emphasis added)

The qualifiers I used for myself at the very beginning of this text are in opposition to things like GATs by virtue of their seeming mutability. How queer, and what is queer anyway? What shade of brown, and whose color guide are we using? How are we defining Chicano here, and how do we determine who gets to count? The persistent desire for consistent classification and categorization, especially those which operate under a binary system, is often a product largely of the Enlightenment and also of the colonial matrix of power. As such, I feel we should exercise caution when placing large amounts of value and validation into the static categories GATs may offer, since this can often reify, at least implicitly, the pro-Whiteness of the colonial matrix of power. With that in mind, there is something to be said for the journey, for the formation of a facet of the self, which empowers one's production of identity deeply and intimately. After all, as Anzaldúa says, "I am the dialogue between my Self and el espiritu del mundo. I change myself, I change the world" (1987: 70).

Israel L. Domínguez is Assistant Professor of Interdisciplinary Studies at Grand Valley State University. His primary research interests focus on decolonization within the context of the U.S.-Mexico borderland religious traditions.

References

Anzaldúa, Gloria (1987). *Borderlands: The New Mestiza = La Frontera.* 1st ed. San Francisco: Spinsters/Aunt Lute.

———. (2015). *Light in the Dark = Luz En Lo Oscuro: Rewriting Identity, Spirituality, Reality*, ed. AnaLouise Keating. Latin America Otherwise: Languages, Empires, Nations. Durham, North Carolina: Duke University Press.

Quijano, Anibal, and Michael Ennis (2000). "Coloniality of Power, Eurocentrism, and Latin America." *Nepantla: Views from South* 1/3: 533–580. https://www.muse.jhu.edu/article/23906

27. The Moves We Make

K. Merinda Simmons

In the flurry of commentary—mostly taking various forms of shock and/or outrage—following Rachel Dolezal's infamous 2015 resignation from the National Association for the Advancement of Colored People (NAACP), one piece stood out, as it questioned the terms of critical engagement. In his June 15, 2015, online piece "From Jenner to Dolezal: One Trans Good, the Other Not So Much," political scientist Adolph Reed, Jr. challenges readers to consider the premises and stakes of self-identification. Pulling no punches, Reed suggests, among other things, that the distinction between what is taken to be trans people's "involuntary" decision and Dolezal's "active choice" "is mind-bogglingly wrong-headed, but it is at the same time thus deeply revealing of the contradictoriness and irrationality that undergird so much self-righteous identitarian twaddle" (Reed 2015). How identitarianism can function ideologically and rhetorically, as Reed describes in his characteristic flourish, is what interests me here.

Only two days after Dolezal formally resigned from the Spokane, WA chapter of the NAACP in June 2015, Dylann Roof shot and killed nine people at the Emanuel African Methodist Episcopal (AME) Church in Charleston, SC. In the wake of the murders, the debate surrounding Dolezal's inglorious resignation from the NAACP seemed comparatively pointless—political small potatoes in a racial landscape still so fraught in the U.S. that even someone as young as twenty-one could be steeped in white supremacy to that degree. Part of me sympathized with the discursive turn away from Dolezal, finding much of the conversation about her scandal exhausting at best. Also easy was to render it frivolous in light of the devastating news out of Charleston. But inasmuch as both events rely upon essentialist understandings of race, they demonstrate how such understandings

SIMMONS *The Moves We Make* 155

operationalize and influence rhetoric on race and, consequently, the ideological choices people make based on that rhetoric. In that sense, the murders at Emanuel AME make the discussion of Rachel Dolezal—i.e., how her phenomenon is made possible and what's at stake in how we talk about that phenomenon—even more pressing.

With that in mind, I found interesting a short BBC feature that was trending online that same summer: "How China debated whether dark or light skin ages better." The piece describes responses out of China to a Harvard study that found Black people to be twice as likely as white people to have a genetic combination resulting in youthful-looking skin. While the study focused on genetic codes across Black and white Americans, it particularly resonated in China, where (like in many other countries, to be sure) traditional definitions of beauty have relied on light skin. And with millions of Chinese citizens taking to the internet to discuss the study, the proclamation of being "Black and proud" arose in what to many might seem like a surprising context (Wendling 2015).

A tiny peek into only one corner of cyberspace banter, the quick BBC write-up is not at all a nuanced discussion of race and identification, of course. All the same, it offers an instructive moment to think about questions of who receives authority to identify as what—when, how, and from whom. Is the donning of "Black is beautiful" rhetoric in China comparable at all to Rachel Dolezal's own self-identification as Black? Or does her situation warrant special critique because of the specific histories of African diasporas in America? And/or because of her role as an activist in the NAACP? When exactly do certain boundaries of identity categories get invoked, policed, and/or reinforced? Obviously, there is never only one answer, nor is there only way to go about answering.

That epistemological multiplicity and ambiguity—as well as the correlative fact that there was not a similar outcry against Caitlyn Jenner's boundary traversal among left-leaning scholarly types—should likewise offer an opportunity to think through some of these questions. Predictable pairings of Dolezal and Jenner have appeared in online commentaries, most chastising the former while celebrating the latter. Academic progressives, especially, who pride ourselves on our commitment to social constructivist views of identity formation,

156 *Fabricating Authenticity*

were surprisingly quick to call out Dolezal's self-identification as disingenuous and praise Jenner's self-awareness. The consistent thread in these responses, of course, is the touting of authenticity. Jenner became who she "really" is, and Dolezal ran away from it, as the stories go, despite the personal performativity in both cases.

While we scholars cling to constructivist talk, it would seem the resonating definition of race remains one tethered to biology, and so the insistence on self-identification that often attends discourse on gender does not apply in matters of racial categories. In this way, Rachel Dolezal called our scholarly bluff. Strict constructivism is simple until someone tries to participate in what that constructivism allows. At that point, the strict policing of the boundaries of identification becomes evident, showcasing the inevitable exclusions within even the seemingly most universalizing ideals. Invocations of personal experience and historical particularity present certain boundaries as categorically uncrossable and others as productively fluid. What this creates in the realm of popular political discourse, of course, is a gaggle of progressive bloggers and talking heads discussing the *real* locus of Black identity and performance, perpetuating romanticized and reductive narratives about "Black America." Joan Walsh's self-congratulatory June 18 Salon piece (2015) is a good example of this phenomenon. Reminding readers of her "own resonance with Black culture," Walsh claims that one of the lessons coming out of the massacre in Charleston is that Dolezal "didn't have to lie to find a home; she just had to work harder to be her true self."

A discussion of how people classify can quickly and easily seem to be merely mind-candy for academic elites, but the Charleston shooting is a prime example of the serious consequences acts of identification carry. In that vein, I am reminded of a story related by Judith Butler about a young man who was killed because of his "feminine" gait. Upon seeing his walk, several other teenage boys antagonize and harass him, ultimately throwing him over a bridge to his death. The sense of threat and panic elicited by this teenager's way of walking reflects the tenuous nature of the normative boundaries he crossed. It is the very contingency of certain boundaries that require their constant policing. As Butler puts it in their now classic *Bodies That Matter: On the Discursive Limits of "Sex,"* "The resignification of norms is thus a function of their *inefficacy*, and so the question of subversion, of *working the weakness in the norm*, becomes a matter of inhabiting the practices of its rearticulation" (1993: 237; emphasis original). Norms and boundaries that articulate dominant notions of gender or race must be tenaciously repeated again and again, as they do not have a stable or inherent substance of their own. We perceive threat when the seams show in our invested presentations of identity categories as clear and experientially or biologically based. After all, part of why so many could so easily embrace Caitlyn Jenner is that she conforms to traditional modes of femininity successfully enough to work a cover of *Vogue*. But to pretend such boundaries are obvious or knowable across time and space is to employ the same destructive logic as those who needed at a physical, visceral level to eradicate the possibility of a man walking with what they deemed a "feminine" style.

Butler calls our attention to the need for a more self-critical use of terminology where identity categories are concerned. Though they are discussing the privileging of being "out," the point is a valuable one when applied to other modes of self-identification as well:

> As much as identity terms must be used, as much as "outness" is to be affirmed, these same notions must become subject to a critique of the exclusionary operations of their own production: For whom is outness an historically available and affordable option? Is there an unmarked class character to the demand for universal "outness"? Who is represented by which use of the term, and who is excluded? For whom does the term present an impossible conflict between racial, ethnic, or religious affiliation and sexual politics? What kinds of policies are enabled by what kinds of usages, and which are backgrounded or erased from view? In this sense, the genealogical critique of the queer subject will be central to queer politics to the extent that it constitutes a self-critical dimension within activism, a persistent reminder to take the time to consider the exclusionary force of one of activism's most treasured contemporary premises. (1993: 227)

When even a walk can be fatal, we should ask what kinds of moves people are allowed to make, both literally and figuratively... who can pass, and who is stopped (at times, dead) in their tracks.

158 *Fabricating Authenticity*

K. Merinda Simmons is Professor of Religious Studies at the University of Alabama. Her books include *Changing the Subject: Writing Women across the African Diaspora* (Ohio State UP, 2014), *The Trouble with Post-Blackness* (co-edited with Houston A. Baker, Jr., Columbia UP, 2015), and *Race and New Modernisms* (co-authored with James A. Crank, Bloomsbury, 2019). She is editor of *Bulletin for the Study of Religion* and of the book series *Concepts in the Study of Religion: Critical Primers*, both with Equinox Publishing Ltd.

References

Butler, Judith (1993). *Bodies That Matter: On the Discursive Limits of "Sex."* New York: Routledge.

Reed, Adolph, Jr. (2015). "From Jenner to Dolezal: One Trans Good, the Other Not So Much." *Common Dreams*, 15 June. Retrieved from https://www.commondreams.org/views/2015/06/15/jenner-dolezal-one-trans-good-other-not-so-much (accessed 25 June 2015).

Walsh, Joan (2015). "No Safe Place to be Black: Charleston and America's Gut-wrenching Racial Truth." *Salon*, 18 June. Retrieved from https://www.salon.com/2015/06/18/no_safe_place_to_be_black_charleston_and_americas_gut_wrenching_racial_truth/ (accessed 25 June 2015).

Wendling, Mike (2015). "How China Debated Whether Dark or Light Skin Ages Better." *BBC News: Trending*, 17 June. Retrieved from https://www.bbc.com/news/blogs-trending-33154841 (accessed 25 June 2015).

28. Trans* Muslims and Jessica Krug: Analyzing the Discursive Power of Authenticity

Hinasahar Muneeruddin

Trans ppl literally worked for the family of our prophet (pbuh) and were given access to spaces that aligned with their gender identities. No amount of uncontextualized hadiths is going to change that.

Trans rights? Sunnah.
Employing trans people? SUNNAH.
Respecting ones gender identity?
S.U.N.N.A.H.
　　　　– Aliyah, @thetranshijabi, on Twitter; August 5, 2020

On September 3, 2020, Jessica A. Krug, (now former) associate professor of History and Africana Studies at George Washington University, publicly confessed to "eschewing [her] lived experience as a white Jewish child [from] suburban Kansas City," claiming instead various identities from "North African Blackness, then U.S. rooted Blackness, then Caribbean rooted Bronx Blackness" (Krug 2020). In fact, throughout her academic career, Krug has identified as "Algerian, African-American, Black Boricua, vaguely Afro-Latinx, vaguely Caribbean; she's been from Kansas City, from the Bronx, and 'of the hood'" paired with "a 'very heavy accent' and an affected brown-girl cool" (Jackson 2020). Krug's claims to Blackness closely resemble the ones Rachel Dolezal made, and in Krug's case, it becomes evident that claims to Blackness became the mechanism

160 *Fabricating Authenticity*

by which to lay claim to an authentic scholarly voice that would not only speak on behalf of the Afro-Caribbean peoples and histories she studies, but also advance her career in academia (Allen 2020).

Building on K. Merinda Simmons' analysis of Dolezal, I examine how Krug's confession also allows us to complicate authenticity and the claims made to approach it. Given the deep-seated, systemic anti-Black racism that the United States was built upon, what harm is being caused when a white person claims Blackness to ensure both recognition and profit? Although it is important to remember that it is difficult and near impossible to locate the sites of "True Authenticity"—it would be absolutely remiss if we do not also consider that while certain claims to authenticity offer space for empowerment (as will be discussed later), other claims (like Krug's and Dolezal's) reify systems of violence and oppression. In other words, even though one cannot discretely determine the boundaries of authenticity, as Simmons maintains, I further argue that an analysis of power structures reveals the inherent violence that is attached to whiteness when it attempts to mark Blackness, and ultimately Black bodies, as their own. In this way, when a white person confesses to posing as a Black person to further their academic career, they not only reify the fungibility (or exchangeability/profitability) of Blackness, but they also remain complicit under the logic of white supremacy—which continues to shape spaces, knowledges, and narratives that were once thought to be amplifying marginalized voices.

While the practical effects of Krug's claims to authenticity drastically differ from those of claims that are strategically employed to empower systemically marginalized voices and identities, they demonstrate the ways in which social actors strategically employ authenticity rhetoric in service of a particular goal (instead of invoking some inherent truth, as is commonly understood). For example, in the case of trans* Muslims, claims to authenticity operate as an explicit strategy taken to step out of liminality and reconcile supposedly "conflicting" identities. In fact, for many trans* Muslims, laying claims to being authentically Muslim does not serve to assert the idea that a monolithic notion of an "Authentic Muslim" actually exists and they fit into that category, but instead, claims to authentic Muslimness are deliberately made in order to open up spaces (discursive and physical) for trans* Muslim safety, community, and survival. The epigraph above is by a Muslim trans*women, Aliyah, who maintains that not only is there historical precedent in affirming trans* identities and rights dating back to the life of Prophet Muhammad, but it also forms a core part of the religion in the form of *Sunnah*, which are understood to be practices and teachings of the Prophet Muhammad that should be emulated as part and parcel of lived religious practice. In much the same way, Aliyah claims authentic Muslimness, be it through citing Islamic authoritative sources like the *Sunnah*, or even with practices such as wearing the hijab. In this way, she reaffirms her Muslim identity as authentic, in the face of all those who attack and threaten her for not being a "true" Muslim, while simultaneously maintaining her gender identity as trans* (Shadijanova 2020). Invoking authentic Muslimness in this way allows trans* Muslims to not only combat normative, exclusionary notions of Muslim practice, but also reclaim their identities from the grasp of patriarchal, cis-heteronormative structures.

Furthermore, although we know that claims to authenticity can configure identities in opposition to each other—if "we" (cis-heterosexuals) are authentically Muslim, then "you" (trans*/nonbinary queer folk) are not—they can also be used as tools for expanding categories of belonging for transformative purposes—if "you" are authentically Muslim, then so am "I." This strategic move upends hegemonic norms and carves out a site of hopeful possibility for trans* Muslims—allowing them to freely exist within it. Ultimately, trans* Muslims' claims to authenticity operate as a way to dismantle the idea of a "Real Thing" or what it means to be an "Authentic Muslim," as mentioned in the Introduction of *Fabricating Authenticity*, without deconstructing the category of "Muslim" into oblivion. This allows trans* Muslims' to claim Muslimness as legitimately as their cis-heterosexual counterparts. Trans* Muslims *re*-construction of what gets to count as Muslim identity through claims of authenticity effectively helps them to not only reclaim lost spaces, identities, communities, but also develop political discourses and use the contests over authenticity for their own mobilization.

In the context of the widespread violence against trans* and queer folk throughout the world, regardless of religion, such

162 *Fabricating Authenticity*

constant affirmations of authenticity ultimately become modes of political empowerment. In fact, trans* Muslims' claims to authentic Muslimness do not relegate violence upon generations of marginalized peoples and bodies like Krug's claims to Blackness/Brownness do. Add to this the vast history in the United States where Muslim Black and Brown bodies have been consistently dehumanized, disciplined, and surveilled (Auston 2018; Khabeer 2016), we can see how one type of claim to authenticity reproduces oppressive systems of cis-heteropatriarchal race-making, while another aims to dismantle it.

Hinasahar Muneeruddin is a doctoral candidate at the University of North Carolina at Chapel Hill in the Islamic Studies track of the Religious Studies program with a graduate certificate in Women and Gender Studies. Hina's research lies at the intersections of islam(s), gender, race, affect, and performativity within the United States. More specifically, she is interested in scenes of gender becoming of Muslims through ritual and spoken word performances.

References

Aliyah (@al1yahal1 & @thetranshijabi) (2020a). "trans rights? Sunnah. employing trans people? SUNNAH. respecting ones gender identity? S. U. N. N. A. H." 5 Aug. 2020, 11:25 PM. *Twitter*. Retrieved from https://twitter.com/al1yahal1/status/1291138332676644864 (access 29 September 2020; website inactive 2024).

———. (2020b). "trans ppl literally worked for the family of our prophet (pbuh)...." 5 Aug. 2020, 11:25 PM. *Twitter*. Retrieved from https://twitter.com/al1yahal1/status/1291138335121879041 (access 29 September 2020; website inactive 2024).

Allen, Charlotte (2020). "Deception and Complicity—the Strange Case of Jessica Krug," *Quillette* (blog), 25 September. Retrieved from https://quillette.com/2020/09/25/deception-and-complicity-the-strange-case-of-jessica-krug/ (accessed 29 September 2020).

Auston, Donna (2017). "Prayer, Protest, and Police Brutality: Black Muslim Spiritual Resistance in the Ferguson Era." *Transforming Anthropology* 25/1: 11–22. https://doi.org/10.1111/traa.12095

Jackson, Lauren Michele (2020). "The Layered Deceptions of Jessica Krug, the Black-Studies Professor Who Hid That She Is White." *The*

New Yorker, 25 September. Retrieved from https://www.newyorker.com/culture/cultural-comment/the-layered-deceptions-of-jessica-krug-the-black-studies-professor-who-hid-that-she-is-white (accessed 29 September 2020).

Khabeer, Su'ad Abdul (2016). *Muslim Cool: Race, Religion, and Hip Hop in the United States.* New York: New York University Press.

Krug, Jessica A. (2020). "The Truth, and the Anti-Black Violence of My Lies." *Medium*, 3 September. Retrieved from https://medium.com/@jessakrug/the-truth-and-the-anti-black-violence-of-my-lies-9a9621401f85 (accessed 29 September 2020).

Shadijanova, Diyora (2020). "Queer Muslims Are Carving Out Their Space On TikTok." *Refinery29*, 6 August. Retrieved from https://www.refinery29.com/en-gb/2020/08/9929540/queer-muslim-tiktok (accessed 29 September 2020).

Afterword: A Little Heritage Goes a Long Way

Andie Alexander and Jason W. M. Ellsworth

Traveling through this book, one thing is for certain: one can find the "authentic" most anywhere. And as we hope this volume has demonstrated, there are a variety of ways that we as humans bring this discourse to life—from Greek cuisine and DNA tests to claims about religious freedom and individualism. At this point, it should by now be clear that "authenticity" is not simply a descriptive label that accurately reflects a "true" quality or inherent aspect of the object or issue in question. Instead, it's a complicated discourse that, when unraveled, tells us much more than initially meets the eye. The one thing that connects with all of the fabrications presented in this book is that of identity—or better yet, as we hope by now you will agree—identification, the performative processes in our lives that establish authority, power, economies, and more. When thinking about "authenticity," one might expect to reveal an essential, original, or accurate quality of something; we instead find a much more complicated set of claims, identities, and power dynamics at stake. The chapters in this volume have offered a range of examples where one could begin unpacking claims of authenticity. But rather than seeing these as distinct case studies that are limited to the data in question, let us apply a few different approaches from the volume to one final extended example.

With one of us having recently lived in Scotland, we thought it a nice opportunity to explore a few seemingly quintessential Scottish examples of authenticity claims at work. So consider this vignette, if you will, of what one would encounter while walking along the Royal Mile in Edinburgh's Old Town. It runs approximately one Scots mile (1.81 km or 0.7 miles) from Edinburgh Castle, which sits atop an ancient volcanic plug, to Holyrood Palace, the official Scottish residence of the British monarch. In addition to its many pubs and shops, the Royal Mile boasts examples of the city's medieval architecture, cobblestone streets, and protected historic buildings—or "listed buildings," to use the official terminology—including buildings such as Parliament Hall, St. Giles' Cathedral, and John Knox House. Listed buildings, which can include a variety of residences or public buildings, are legally recognized as places of special interest to Scottish (and British) history, architecture, and culture. Countries within the UK each have their own historic agency which grades, or ranks, buildings based on the historic quality—i.e., how representative it is of a particular period or style—and national significance of the building. These grades also determine how much and to what extent listed structures can be modified and updated so as to "preserve" and protect these sites of Scottish heritage. Accordingly, any changes or updates must be approved by a few organizations and planning authorities. While lower-grade listings might allow additions and modifications suited to modern living, buildings with higher grades require "historically accurate" construction methods and materials, paint colors, and structure maintenance (British Listed Buildings n.d.). The preservation of these sites hinges on notions of historic and architectural authenticity outlined by British government agencies. Yet, even buildings with the highest grade have been updated with modern conveniences such as indoor plumbing, electricity, heating, and modern kitchens, so there are clearly some exceptions to the rule. This is not to say that building conservation is somehow hypocritical—not at all. Instead, we can see that the claims of historic and architectural authenticity are very much a strategic national project—rather than objective evidence—which helps to construct a particular narrative of Scottish heritage and sense of national identity.

While exploring the architectural nuances of the historic buildings along the Mile, you may find yourself ready to stop for a meal at one of the variety of pubs offering "authentic" Scottish meals—after all, you can't go to Scotland without trying its national dish, haggis, and perhaps washing it down with a cold bottle of Irn-Bru, a bright orange Scottish soda—or what they might call "fizzy juice" or simply "juice"—which is reported to be Scotland's "other national

166 *Fabricating Authenticity*

drink"—after whisky, of course. For those who aren't familiar, haggis is sheep's stomach filled with innards, oatmeal, onions, and spices. Haggis is generally understood to be a Scottish dish, but the origins of the dish are less clear. There are several accounts of how it may have come to Scotland from the Vikings, ancient Rome, or, perhaps, England (Lee 2019). But it was the English who first categorized this dish as "Scottish." By the later 1700s, haggis was but one way the English would attempt to portray the Scottish as heathens, as uncivilized (ibid.). But Scottish poet Robert Burns reframed that narrative in his well-known "Address to a Haggis." Following his verse disparaging continental European cuisine, Burns further claims it is insufficient, leaving men weak and feeble:

> Poor devil! See him owre [over] his trash,
> As feckless [feeble] as a wither'd rash [reed],
> His spindle-shank [skinny leg] a guid whip-lash,
> His nieve [fist] a nit [nut]....

Whereas haggis, as Burns continues, was the food for *real men*:

> But mark the Rustic [healthy], haggis-fed,
> The trembling earth resounds his tread,
> Clap in his walie nieve [strong fist] a blade,
> He'll mak it whissle [work].... (Burns 1787)

So, unlike the English and Europeans, Scottish men were made strong and fearsome with their "rustic" diet of haggis. Burns' poem cemented haggis' place in Scottish history and identity, and it remains an integral part of the traditional meal served on Burns Night, an annual celebration of the poet and an important event of Scottish heritage and culture (Scottish Parliament 2017). Haggis, then, is an excellent example of how competing narratives are used to establish boundaries and construct a group identity and heritage.

While the origins of haggis are rather unclear, Scotland's famous Irn-Bru (originally Iron Brew) is claimed to have stronger ties to the country, though there may be some discrepancy about its origins. The first documented "Iron Brew" was sold by a Scottish family in Kingston, Jamaica in 1891, but that beverage was made with mass-produced concentrates which were sold by a company from New York, Maas & Waldstein, who are "credited as the true historical originators" of the fizzy drink now known as Irn-Bru (Leishman 2017: 5). Maas & Waldstein first sold their carbonated soft drink IRONBREW in 1889 as "the ideal American drink" (ibid.: 6). Across the Atlantic, there were several competing claims to the drink's origins in England, but most notably, the Scottish company A. G. Barr began selling what we now know as Irn-Bru in 1898, and officially launching in 1901, the original label pictured a Highland Games athlete (ibid.: 8, 10–11). Aiming to offer Scottish laborers an alternative to beer, the drink was marketed as a strong drink for strong, working-class laborers (A. G. Barr n.d.). However, following WWII, the UK established "new food labelling regulations which insisted that brand names should be 'literally true,'" and since the soft drink didn't contain iron and wasn't brewed, the company had to change the name (Leishman 2017: 12). In 1946, the company trademarked their new name "Irn-Bru," which distinguished it from other soft drinks on the market as well as other *generic* Iron Brew beverages. Not only did the new name sound just like the old one while also meeting the new regulations, but its spelling made it easily identifiable and distinctively Scottish, as it reflects the Glaswegian pronunciation of the earlier name (ibid.: 13–14). In 1988, Irn-Bru released a big-budget ad—not unlike that of Coca-Cola—which "parodied U.S. advertising tropes" while also highlighting the drink's Scottish roots and thereby linking it to Scottish national identity (ibid.). As sung in the 1988 ad:

> It's not a drink from those crazy Yanks
> Because it's made right here
> You know it's tougher than tanks.
>
> Made in Scotland from girders,
> Unpronounceable too.
> Made in Scotland from girders,
> It's called Barr's Irn-Bru?

The song in the 1988 ad denounces any connections Irn-Bru might have with the "crazy Yanks" in the U.S. and fabricates the national narrative of the hardy, Scottish drink's key ingredient, girders (i.e.,

168 *Fabricating Authenticity*

large iron or steel beams), as imbuing it the strength of the steel workers..., or being "the very nectar" of Glasgow Central Station's steel beams..., or claiming that girder extract is what gives the drink its distinctive rusty color... (The Newsroom 2016). While the exact function of girders may remain a mystery, they have played a key role in both establishing the Scottishness of the drink while also creating a sense of national identity. Today, Irn-Bru is the top-selling soda in Scotland and is understood to be a product that's unique to Scotland. This is evidenced, in part, by the on-going discussions that try to determine the flavor of the drink. Comments range from claiming that it tastes like the color orange, to being some combination of ginger, banana extract, and bubblegum, to having somewhat of a metallic taste (Billet 2023). The purported incomparability of the drink helps to foster a sense of Scottish distinction and uniqueness from both the bright orange color to the ambiguous flavor that is simply "strong and Scottish." The drink is very much a staple in Scotland, and it works—in some small way—to create a particular shared identity. After all, Irn-Bru even has its own tartan. What could be more Scottish?

Rejoining the bustling Royal Mile after a nice meal and a chance to rest your legs, you'll find a good many shops selling all sorts of Scottish souvenirs, and amid all the hairy coos (that is, Highland cows), thistles, and whisky is a world of tartan and shops selling tailored "authentic" Scottish kilts. If you don't want to splurge on the authentic kilt, you can easily find just about any article of clothing or accessory in a variety of tartan patterns and color combinations. In addition to the immense variety, every shop will also have a space allocated for clan-specific apparel, which is limited to a handful of the more prominent or popular clans. And while there are plenty tartan varieties to strike anyone's fancy, the set-apart clan-specific tartans create a sense of distinction and authenticity, particularly for the consumer. For those who claim Scottish ancestry, the clan-specific tartans help foster a sense of heritage or tradition specific to that family. But what is that heritage and where did those traditions originate?

Kilts have become an iconic symbol of Scottish identity, but that was not always the case. While there are different historical accounts of where Medieval Scots originate, some argue that they were historically and culturally Irish. And at the time, Highlanders wore a long tunic (*léine*, in Scots Gaelic) like the Irish. Kilts, like the ones worn today, did not emerge until much later (as famously argued by Trevor-Roper [1992: 19]). The precursor to the modern kilt is the great kilt, or belted plaid (*féileadh mór*, in Scots Gaelic—not to be conflated with the linguistically similar Irish Gaelic, or Gaelic as it's more widely known, which is either a distinct dialect or different language entirely, depending on who you ask [yet another site of authenticity discourses at work]). Popular examples of the belted plaid appear in the 1995 film *Braveheart* and the recent TV series *Outlander*. However, it is worth noting that the belted plaid first appeared in the sixteenth century, nearly 300 years after William Wallace, and clan-specific tartans—like the one occasionally worn by *Outlander*'s protagonist, Jamie Fraser (Moore 2014)—weren't established until the late-eighteenth century, well after the Battle of Culloden in 1746. Moreover, the modern kilt was invented in the 1720s by Thomas Rawlinson, a Quaker from Lancashire, England. So how did the kilt become a symbol of ancient Scottish heritage?

Following the 1707 union of Scotland and England into one kingdom, a series of Scottish Jacobite uprisings aimed to restore the House of Stuart to the British monarchy—the most notable was the 1745 rebellion (or the Forty-five Rising), which ended with the English victory at the Battle of Culloden in 1746. In response to the uprisings, the British Parliament issued the 1746 Act of Proscription which attempted to disband the Highland culture and assimilate the Scottish. One such Act was the 1746 Dress Act which outlawed all forms of Highland dress, *including the kilt*. The Act carried a punishment of six months' imprisonment for the first offense; the second offense resulted in transportation to British plantations overseas for seven years (Trevor-Roper 1992: 24). After thirty-five years, the Act was repealed in 1782 with the help of the Highland Society of London, a group who fabricated and romanticized an ancient Highland culture to then preserve. The once "vulgar," "servile," and "low class" clothing (ibid.: 24–25, 28) became a romanticized "celebration of the untamed wilderness" of Scotland, and Highlanders were no longer "dangerous, barelegged barbarians," but instead an "admirable... kilted version of the 'noble savage'" (Bolton 2004).

170 *Fabricating Authenticity*

The kilt was further cemented as the Scottish national dress in 1822 with George IV's carefully managed state visit to Edinburgh where he appeared in Highland dress. Sir Walter Scott convinced the Scottish chieftains and clans to come dressed in their newly established clan tartans for the royal visit (Trevor-Roper 1992: 29–31). George IV's own red tartan kilt would later become the Royal Stuart tartan. On the one hand, this could be understood as an English monarch showing deference to Scottish history or celebrating Scottish culture. But it is important to consider the variety of power dynamics at work in this particular event. Given that the British ban of Highland dress was an explicit attempt to manage and domesticate the Scottish clans, the fact that the most prominent reappearance of the kilt was both by and in service of the first royal visit in Edinburgh following the 1745 rebellion is not insignificant. What was once a "symbol of rebellion and primitive savagery" (Bolton 2004) is thus rebranded as fashionable attire for Scottish nobility in Britain—nobility who are loyal to the Crown. The once minimally colored, inexpensive garments now boast a variety of detailed patterns and bright colors. Where the belted plaid had been a long full-length garment that allowed for more mobility for laborers, provided warmth, and shielded the wearer from harsh weather, the modern kilt, invented by Thomas Rawlinson, is effectively the bottom half of the belted plaid that is smaller and tailored with the back pleats already sewn in—more suited for fashion than function, perhaps.

The popularity of kilts continued among the British aristocracy, which resulted in the establishment of appropriate styles and settings for either daytime or evening kilts (ibid.). Although the kilt is now widely recognized as a symbol of Scottish heritage and identity, it is also very much a British—or rather, English—construct which, implicitly or explicitly, aids in asserting and maintaining British authority over Scotland. Ultimately, the kilt has been successfully domesticated and rebranded to provide what we now might understand as the illusion of a distinct ancient Scottish heritage and identity while simultaneously integrating the Scottish clans as part of the British kingdom (see Lincoln 1989). This integration does not curtail tension or dissent; rather, it creates a space wherein Scottish identity can be asserted but without threatening—and in some sense, reifying—the power and stability of the British government (see McCutcheon 2005; Stack et al. 2015).

The early belted plaids were not clan-specific in their design or coloring. Color differentiation was more a mark of status or authority. The plaids of clan chieftains were colored whereas their followers' plaids were brown (Trevor-Roper 1992: 23). Prior to the royal visit in 1822, differentiated clan tartans were gaining popularity as a result of the work of Sir Walter Scott, and in 1819, the Highland Society of London began certifying clan tartans. The certification lent a sense of authenticity and respectability to the clans, which, in turn, created a market for establishing and certifying clan tartans (ibid.: 30). While George IV's visit revitalized the tartan industry, the widespread popularization of tartans both in Scotland and internationally is, in large part, due to Queen Victoria's romanticization of Scotland—or what is referred to as "Balmorality," named for her Scottish residence Balmoral Castle.

In 1852, Queen Victoria and Prince Albert commissioned Balmoral Castle in Aberdeenshire, near the Highlands, which firmly established an English royal presence in the former Jacobite estate (ibid.: 38). Victoria and Albert were particularly fond of Scottish dress and tartans—creating a number of tartan patterns themselves. The castle decor also reflected their love of tartan, and Victoria's penchant for tartan clothing helped introduce tartan into women's fashion more broadly creating a Victorian tartan revival (Stern 2013; Fiddes n.d.). And along with the writings of Sir Walter Scott, Queen Victoria's romanticization of the Highland lifestyle and beauty reframed Scotland on the international stage helping establish it as a tourist destination (Chanter 2017). Today, you need only stroll down Edinburgh's Royal Mile to see how the fabrication of Scottish heritage has created a thriving modern tourism industry. And now with ancestry and DNA tests there's an even greater interest in learning about one's distant heritage.

While clan tartan might be limited in the souvenir shops, one can more readily find Scottish clan history books. These are short little books that tell *The Origins of the [Clan] and Their Place in History*. Each book features the clan tartan and crest on the cover and then opens with the clan motto, the territories where the clan(s) are located, and clan name variations. After outlining the nebulous origins of the

172 *Fabricating Authenticity*

clan, the book provides some scattered references to the clan throughout Scottish history, beginning with the reign of James VI and I of Scotland and England. The book concludes with a list of people with the clan name who have "gained international acclaim" (Gray 2019: 25). Though the books tell the history of the clans in general, broad strokes—however minor their historical role may have been—they provide enough relevant historical detail for the reader to develop a sense of connection with the clan and authorize their own narrative of Scottish heritage and sense of identity within that framework.

In light of this discussion of Scottish tartans and kilts, consider this one final example. On 26 March 2023, the Scottish Tartans Authority (STA) announced that a piece of tartan found in a peat bog—a wetland containing thousands of years of partially decayed plant material (peat), which is a key component in many of the whiskies produced in Scotland's western isles—in Glen Affric in the 1980s is, in fact, the "oldest known piece of *true* tartan discovered in Scotland" (BBC 2023; emphasis added). Following recent dye analysis and radiocarbon dating, the STA learned that the fabric was created sometime between 1500–1600. Though the "Falkirk 'tartan'" dates from the third century CE, it has "a simpler check pattern woven using undyed yarns" (V&A Dundee 2023). The STA posits that while the Glen Affric tartan might be able to provide greater historical insight on the types of wool and dyes that were used in creating early tartans—perhaps even where they come from—, it ultimately provides more questions than answers. Peter MacDonald, Head of Research and Collections at the STA, further reifies the idea of authentic tartan when he explains that "tartan has several colours with multiple stripes of different sizes, [which] corresponds to what people would think of as a true tartan" (V&A Dundee 2023). This discovery, according to MacDonald, "proves … that the tartan tradition has continued from at least the 16th century to today." And he hopes to "recreate the tartan, matching the colours to how they would've appeared centuries ago" (Vermes 2023).

This discovery, and the new technology that made it possible, help create a more robust history of tartan and its use in Scottish history, particularly since the eradication of Highland dress erased much of that history. But, as you also may be wondering, what is this "true"

ALEXANDER AND ELLSWORTH *Afterword* 173

Scottish tartan, and how is that authenticity gauged, particularly given the apparent lack of historical information that we have. Perhaps more importantly, why is there even such an emphasis on it being a "true Scottish tartan"? How might we accurately determine the original colors? Do the same plants, from which the dyes were derived, still grow in the region? How rich or dull might they have been? How did the dyes interact with the wool of sixteenth century sheep? How were the colors affected by diet and climate? The list goes on and on. And we hope by now that such assertions stand out a bit more and start bringing a variety of questions to mind. It's certainly no accident that this claim was made on a variety of media outlets, so what might be at stake in establishing this longer heritage of Scottish tartan given what we now know of its contested history in the United Kingdom?

We can see that authenticity claims are very much at work in the discourses regarding the new information about the Glen Affric tartan. While this is undoubtedly a notable addition to the historical record and an excellent example of how scientific advancement makes this knowledge possible, we must also critically consider how the presentation of the new information in this narrative of Scottish history actively works to construct a sense of an ancient Scottish heritage and national identity. So what might we make of this interview about the Glen Affric tartan with Peter MacDonald by CBC Radio's *As It Happens* co-host Nil Köksal:

KÖKSAL: It's such an incredible and beautiful tradition—history and families and clans woven into these fabrics. You mentioned the size of the weave, the type of weave, and what that suggests to you, but what colors would we see when we look at this fabric?

MACDONALD: So we're looking at a tartan that was probably red and yellow or tan within overstrikes of green and black/brown on it.

KÖKSAL: Has it been connected to a particular clan?

MACDONALD: Yes and no. [laughs] Let's start with the "no" bit first: that's because the concept of clan tartans is an early nineteenth

174   *Fabricating Authenticity*

century one. Before that, people wore what they liked or could afford or what was available—it's a combination of all of those things. And the better off would have always wanted better colors, better quality, etc. So it wouldn't have been directly associated with a clan. ... It's a hugely important piece because it's so early, because it's like a transitional piece that talks to us about the early development of tartan in Scotland, and also, it's a way of linking back and reaching into the past and making that connection with the later clan tartans. ... It's a piece of national importance and significance.

KÖKSAL: Beyond the national significance, for those from abroad— maybe from Canada—who come to visit the [V&A Dundee] museum, what story do you hope it tells them?

MACDONALD: Well, it links very nicely with the Scots diaspora, and a lot of the Highland Scots went [to] Canada [in] the eighteenth and nineteenth centuries. And only last year, I was up in Prince Edward Island (PEI) for the 200th anniversary of the Gauls who went into PEI and took with them a piece of tartan that had been worn at Culloden in 1746—taken there in 1772—to go there and see that, and that [almost brings] it full circle. (MacDonald and Köksal 2023)

At first glance, tartan might appear to be little more than a simple piece of colored fabric, but as we have seen, it is intricately woven into the social processes of fabricating notions of identity, nationality, and heritage—processes that are continually recreated and redefined by various sets of relationships and claims as the examples throughout this volume have demonstrated. Much like claims to heritage, history, tradition, and origins, a claim of authenticity is therefore not an "accurate" representation or preservation of a clearly defined historical quality or moment. Rather, it is a discourse that is negotiated in the present; it is used to organize—and importantly *authorize*—our understandings of our current identities and social worlds. Authenticity rhetoric, then, is an effective method for both justifying certain power dynamics or challenging them; for selling a product or service as a way of life; or to make others invisible or shine a light on those being ignored. Claims of authenticity create and prioritize competing hierarchies—it just depends on who's wielding it and how convincing their narrative is.

From tartan and the Royal Mile to haggis and Irn-Bru, along with the broader set of claims to Scottish authenticity bundled together, we hope this example demonstrates how one might begin rethinking historical relations of power and identity. From colonial to capitalist powers, we find an interconnected set of discourses that are established in a variety of manners, all having a practical effect in the present. And while the stakes may be seemingly higher with certain claims or at discrete moments and in specific situations, there are similarities to how one unpacks the claims of authenticity circulating around the bottle of wine that you picked up on the way home from work today or the Coca-Cola that you just grabbed from a vending machine. What at first sight is a mundane stroll down a bookstore aisle browsing for a self-help book or a walk along an old road selling trinkets to tourists, a closer look allows us to unravel the fabric that we as humans have woven to construct our world. So the next time you go for a walk, keep your chin up as you never know what you might bump into.

Andie Alexander is a doctoral candidate in the Institute for the Study of Religion at Leibniz University Hannover and is Managing Editor of *The Religious Studies Project*. Her research focuses on identity construction, discourses of difference and experience, and conceptions of the individual as a way of examining how post-9/11 discourses of inclusivity and pluralism implicitly work as a form of governance and subject-making which construct and constrain the liberal Muslim subject.

Jason W. M. Ellsworth is a doctoral candidate in the Sociology and Social Anthropology Department at Dalhousie University. He currently works at the Faculty of Medicine at the University of Prince Edward Island and serves on the Executive Committee of the Canadian Anthropology Society. His research explores a diverse array of topics including the Anthropology and Sociology of Religion, Buddhism in North America, Food and Food Movements, Theories of Value, Political Economy, Marketing, Transnationalism, and Orientalism.

176   *Fabricating Authenticity*

References

A. G. Barr (n.d.). "Irn Bru," *AG Barr*. Retrieved from https://www.agbarr. co.uk/our-brands/barr-soft-drinks/irn-bru/ (accessed 30 March 2023).

Barr's Irn-Bru (1988). "Made in Scotland from Girders." YouTube video, 01:00. Posted 8 September 2008. Retrieved from https://www.youtube. com/watch?v=H4PxuFQCDis (accessed 30 March 2023).

BBC News (2023). "Oldest Tartan Found to Date Back to 16th Century." *BBC News*, 26 March. Retrieved from https://www.bbc.co.uk/news/uk-scotland-65081312 (accessed 30 March 2023).

Billet, Alexander (2023). "What Exactly Is Irn-Bru, And What Does It Taste Like?" *Daily Meal*, 12 July. https://www.thedailymeal.com/1337691/irn-bru-soda-flavor-explained/ (accessed 15 July 2023).

Bolton, Andrew (2004). "The Kilt," In *Heilbrunn Timeline of Art History*, October. New York: The Metropolitan Museum of Art, 2000–. https:// www.metmuseum.org/toah/hd/kilt/hd_kilt.htm

British Listed Buildings (n.d.). "What Are Listed Buildings?" *British Listed Buildings*. Retrieved from https://britishlistedbuildings.co.uk/site/about-listed-buildings/#.ZCDG3uzMKeA (accessed 30 March 2023).

Burrns, Robert (1787) [2000]. "An Address to a Haggis." *In The Complete Poems and Songs of Robert Burns*. Glasgow: The Gresham Publishing Company.

Chanter, Rachel (2017). "Balmorality: The Romanticisation of Scotland," *Peter Harrington Journal – The Journal*. 11 September. Retrieved from https://www.peterharrington.co.uk/blog/balmorality-the-romanticisation-of-scotland/ (accessed 30 March 2023).

Fiddes, Nick (n.d.). "The Influence of Queen Victoria and Walter Scott on the Popularity of the Kilt in the 19th Century." *CLAN*. https://clan.com/help/kilts-origins-history-today/kilts-queen-victoria-walter-scott (accessed 30 March 2023).

Gray, Iain (2019). *Rae: The Origins of the Raes and Their Place in History*. Lang Syne Publishers Ltd.

Hobsbawm, Eric (1992). "Introduction: Inventing Traditions." In Eric Hobsbawm and Terence Ranger (eds.), *The Invention of Tradition*, 1–14. Cambridge: Cambridge University Press. https://doi.org/10.1017/CBO9781107295636.001

Lee, Alexander (2019). "A History of Haggis." *History Today* 69/12. Retrieved from https://www.historytoday.com/archive/historians-cookbook/history-haggis (accessed 30 March 2023).

Leishman, David (2017). "'Original and Best'? How Barr's Irn-Bru Became a Scottish Icon." *Études Écossaises* 19: 1–18. https://doi.org/10.4000/etudesecossaises.1206

ALEXANDER AND ELLSWORTH *Afterword* 177

Lincoln, Bruce (1989). *Discourse and the Construction of Society: Comparative Studies of Myth, Ritual, and Classification*. New York and Oxford: Oxford University Press.

MacDonald, Peter, and Köksal, Nil (2023). "World's Oldest-Known Surviving Scottish Tartan Has 'More to Tell,' Says Researcher." *As It Happens*. CBC Radio, 29 March. Retrieved from https://www.cbc.ca/listen/live-radio/1-2-as-it-happens/clip/15975288-worlds-oldest-known-surviving-scottish-tartan-more-tell-says (accessed 30 March 2023).

McCutcheon, Russell T. (2005). *Religion and the Domestication of Dissent: Or, How to Live in a Less than Perfect Nation*. Sheffield, UK: Equinox Publishing Ltd.

Moore, Ronald D., creator (2014). *Outlander*. Left Bank Pictures, Tall Ship Productions, and Story Mining & Supply Co. Starz.

Scottish Parliament (2017). "Celebrating Burns and the Scots Language." *The Scottish Parliament / Pàrlamaid na h-Alba*, 25 January. Retrieved from https://www.scottishparliament.tv/meeting/celebrating-burns-and-the-scots-language-january-25-2017 (accessed 30 March 2023).

Stack, Trevor, Naomi R. Goldenberg, and Timothy Fitzgerald (eds.) (2015). *Religion as a Category of Governance and Sovereignty*. Leiden: Brill.

Stern, L. R. (2013). "Balmorality: Queen Victoria's Tartan Craze," *Plaid Petticoats* (blog), 11 March. Retrieved from http://plaidpetticoats.blogspot.com/2013/03/balmorality-queen-victorias-tartan-craze.html (accessed 30 March 2023).

The Newsroom (2016). "Is Irn-Bru Really Made from Girders." *The Scotsman*, 9 June. Retrieved from https://www.scotsman.com/arts-and-culture/is-irn-bru-really-made-from-girders-1474787 (accessed 30 March 2023).

Trevor-Roper, Hugh (1992). "The Invention of Tradition: The Highland Tradition of Scotland." In Eric Hobsbawm and Terence Ranger (eds.), *The Invention of Tradition*, 15–41. Cambridge: Cambridge University Press. https://doi.org/10.1017/CBO9781107295636.002

V&A Dundee (2023). "Scotland's Oldest Tartan Discovered by Scottish Tartans Authority." *V&A Dundee*, 26 March. Retrieved from https://www.vam.ac.uk/dundee/info/scotland-s-oldest-tartan-discovered-by-scottish-tartans-authority (accessed 30 March 2023).

Vermes, Jason (2023). "World's Oldest-Known Surviving Scottish Tartan Has 'More to Tell,' Says Researcher." *CBC Radio*, 29 March. Retrieved from https://www.cbc.ca/radio/asithappens/worlds-oldest-scottish-tartan-1.6793911 (accessed 30 March 2023).

Index

1746 Act of Proscription, 169
2020 Uprising, 76, 97–8

ADHD, 120–1
advertisement, 7–8, 140, 145–6
  as manipulative, 41
  parody of, 167–8
  as trend, 39, 41–2, 155
  See also marketing
A. G. Barr, 167
Alexander, Andie, ix, 74, 80, 115,
  117–19
Aliyah, 159, 161
anachronism, 102, 105, 107, 110
ancestry, 144–7, 151, 171
  as heritage, 150, 168
Antifa, 76, 99
Anzaldúa, Gloria, 149–52
Appadurai, Arjun, 47
appropriation, 12, 80, 141, 146,
  151, 156
AR-15s, 92–3
art, 10, 23, 25, 27, 46, 49, 59–60,
  63, 117, 139
  adaptations of, 103–4
  aura of, 138
  as high vs. low art, 42, 117
  forgery, 112–15
  mass production of, 10–11
  restoration, 104, 112–15, 117–18

  See also fashion; forgery; luxury;
    restoration
attention, 117–22
  inattention, 119–21
  ritual attention, 119
authenticity
  as category, 1, 3, 5–6, 13, 24,
    30–2, 34–7, 135, 161, 164
  claims and discourses of, 1–2, 6,
    10–13, 21–2, 24, 27, 32, 35–7,
    41–2, 49, 66–8, 84, 87, 89–90,
    103, 109–10, 114, 117–18,
    121–2, 132, 135, 138, 141–2,
    156–7, 160–2, 164, 169, 173–5
  as contested, 12, 31–2, 35–6,
    93–4, 121, 139–40, 146
  as essence, 4, 39, 42, 156, 164
  as genuine, 1–2, 9–11, 30, 32,
    42–3, 60, 84, 115
  and hyperreality, 27–8
  as original, 1, 7, 9–10, 18, 21, 23,
    24–5, 27, 31, 37, 104, 112–15,
    117, 127, 137, 150, 164, 166–8,
    171, 173–4
  as real, 1–2, 4–11, 30, 32, 36, 40,
    88–90, 109, 114, 131–4, 135–6,
    146, 156, 161, 166
  as sincere, 8, 21, 104, 121–2
  spectre of authenticity, 12
  as totalitarian state, 35

Index 179

as true, 1, 4–5, 11, 36, 39, 42, 88, 113, 133, 147, 156, 161, 164, 167, 172–3
authority
    as constructed, 1, 4–7, 10, 21, 23, 24–5, 27, 51–3, 84, 104, 114, 128–9, 155, 172
    as gendered, 51–3, 127–9
    structures of, x, 52, 81, 119–20, 133, 136, 142, 147, 161, 164, 170, 174

Backer, Bill, 7–9
Baldrick-Morrone, Tara, 54–5, 57
Barker, Travis, 61
Battle of Culloden, 169
Baudrillard, Jean, 27
Baumgartner Fine Art Restoration (BFAR), 113
Bayart, Jean-François, ix–x, 1, 3, 10, 40–1, 47
Bendix, Regina, 11–12
Benjamin, Walter, 45–6, 138
bias
    gender bias, 52–3. *See also* gender
    as implicit, 52–3, 54
    media bias, 71, 76, 97. *See also* media
Bible, the, 93, 102, 118, 120, 126, 133
    as e-Bible, 119
biological essentialism
    and identity, 144–7, 151, 157
    racism of, 146–7
    rhetoric of, 145
    See also ethnicity; race; racism
Black Lives Matter movement, 76
Blackness, 54, 61, 64, 76, 98, 155–6, 159–60, 162
    anti-Black racism, 160

Black Israelites, 73–4, 79
Black-led resistance, 68
commodification of, 160
and strategic individuality, 79–80
    See also racism
Blink-182, 61
Bo.Lan, 24–5
boundary formation, 22–3, 150, 156
    boundary crossing, 150, 155–6
    boundary policing, 2, 42, 60, 109, 132, 156
    as hierarchy or power, 2, 38, 42, 45–7, 66–7, 74–5, 80, 94, 127–8, 157, 160, 169–70
    as identity construction, 39, 42, 155–6, 160–1, 166
    as othering, 109
    study of, 2, 7
Bourdieu, Pierre, 47, 49, 60
Buddhism
    as classification, 108–10, 137
    Diamond Way Buddhism, 137
Burns, Robert, 166
Bush, Billy, 83
Butler, Judith, 73, 156–7

Canada, 19–20, 30–2, 65, 67, 139, 142, 173–4
    Prince Edward Island (PEI), 30–2, 174
    Toronto, 18, 87
cancel culture, 75–6, 97, 99
capitalism, 9, 11, 41, 45, 47–9, 63–6, 84–5
    hegemony of, 141
    racial capitalism, 64, 66–7, 98
    philanthrocapitalism, 63–4, 67
    settler colonial-capitalism, 67–8, 140, 175
Carpenter, John, 42; *They Live* (film)

180 *Fabricating Authenticity*

categories. *See* classification
Cavanaugh v. Bartelt (2016), 132
Chang, David, 34–8
charity, 60–1, 64, 68, 140, 142
    charity law, 135, 137–8, 139
    as philanthropy, 60–1, 63, 142
Charity Commission of England
    and Wales (CC), 135–8
Charleston, SC, 154, 156
Charlottesville, VA, 144
Chef's Table (TV series), 24–5
China
    beauty standards, 155
    Chinese food, 5, 20, 30
    Hong Kong, 46–7
Christ, Stephen, 31–2
Christianity
    as baby Christian, 83–5
    as Catholicism, 125–7, 133
    as Charismatic Christianity,
        118–22
    as classification, 76, 83–5, 93–4,
        132–3, 139, 142
    as conservative, 74, 76
    as cult, 92–3
    Evangelicals, 83
    hegemony of, 81, 85, 92–4,
        137–8, 139–40, 142
    as identity, 93, 125–9
    as Protestantism, 61, 81, 125
Church of the Flying Spaghetti
    Monster, 131–4
classification
    as branding, 2, 9, 39, 84–5, 137,
        140–1, 167, 170
    complexity of, 1, 5–6, 12–13,
        17–19, 27, 35–7, 46, 49, 80,
        92–4, 96, 102, 108, 118, 146,
        152, 157
    as exclusionary, 46, 80, 120–1,
        136, 156–7, 161

politics of, 75–6, 97–100, 144–5,
    167
power of, 1–2, 127–8, 152, 160–1
processes, 1, 11–12, 32, 35, 84–5,
    89–90, 154–7
as strategic, 3, 40, 46, 51, 66–7,
    79–80, 85, 89, 92–4, 109–10,
    127–8, 136–8, 139–40, 164,
    166
Clooney, George, 103
Coca-Cola, 1, 7–9, 14, 39, 43, 167,
    175
    Diet Coke, 39, 43
    vs. Pepsi, 8, 43
Coleman, Simon, 37
colonialism, 67, 151, 175
    colonial-capitalist state apparatus,
        68, 98, 140–1
    colonial matrix of power, 152
    and erasure of heritage, 151, 169
    as European, 98–9, 150
    as Manifest Destiny, 98–9
    settler-colonialism, 67–8, 74
    See also capitalism; ideology
commodity, 5–11, 40, 46
    commodity fetishism, 40–3,
        48–9, 165–8
    and identity construction, 11, 40,
        49
    systems of commodification, 67,
        114, 160
    and value, 40, 49, 56
comparison, 2, 6, 11–12, 32, 53,
    168
consumerism
    as anti-consumerist, 9
    as conspicuous consumption, 47,
        49
    as ethical consumption, 141
    identity as consumer, 10, 39–42,
        47–9

Index 181

as performative, 48–9
product-consumer relationship, 9, 11, 31–2, 35–7, 40, 45–7, 168
Cook, Roger, 7–9
cookbooks, 5–6, 18, 22. *See also* food
cosmetics. *See* makeup, power dynamics of
Cotter, Christopher R., 48–9
Coulthard, Glen, 67
COVID-19, 34, 45
impact on education, 54–8
Covington High School, 71, 73–4, 81
cult, 92–4
Culture on the Edge, ix–x, 2, 13

Davis, Angela, 68, 97–8
Davis, Billy, 7
description
as meaning-making, x, 23, 88–9, 92–3, 102–4, 164
as strategic essentialism, 8, 53, 54–5, 79–81, 85, 92–3, 97–8, 133, 164
Devine, Patricia, 52–3
difference
as boundary formation, 47, 66–7, 94
as fabricated, 8–9, 47, 89, 94, 114, 147, 151
Disneyland, 27–28
Wizarding World of Harry Potter, 27
DNA Discussion Project, 145
DNA testing. *See* GATs (genetic ancestry testing)
Dobson, James, 83, 85
Dolezal, Rachel, 154–6, 159–60
dolmas, 16–19, 23
as *dolmades*, 19

Drake (Aubrey Graham), 59–61, 63–4, 68

Ecce Homo, 112–15
Ellsworth, Jason W. M., ix, 35–6, 74, 80, 92
England, 135, 166–7, 169–70, 172
Esposito, Raffaele, 25–6
essentialism
as socially constructed, 6, 23, 31, 145
strategic essentialism, 4, 72, 76, 79–80, 154
See also biological essentialism
Estes, Nick, 67
ethnicity, 7, 31, 51
as category, 146
as Chicanx, 149, 152
as Latinx, 81, 149–51, 159
as mestizx, 149–50
as minority or marginalized group, 128, 146, 157
and power dynamics, 127–8, 157
See also classification; race; racism; tradition
experience
as constructed, 11, 24, 27, 30–2, 36–7, 46, 56–7, 90
as fetishized, 32
as personal, 156
as socially contingent, 45, 52, 107, 119, 142, 146
See also memory

F for Fake (film), 114–15
Family Guy (TV series) 79–80
Farmers of Wine, 9–10
fashion, 42, 48
as identity construction, 8, 141, 168–72
as low art, 42

182 *Fabricating Authenticity*

name-brand, 10, 46–8
See also art; commodity; luxury
feminism, 88, 149
Fillitz, Thomas and Saris, A. Jamie, 12
Fitzgerald, Timothy, 40, 43
Focus on the Family, 83. *See also* Dobson, James
food
  as authentic, 5–6, 11, 24–7, 30–1, 35–7
  as class-based, 42, 165–6
  as cultural/national cuisine, 3, 5–6, 16–19, 20, 24–5, 30–2, 35–6, 165–6
  globalization of, 5–6, 30
  and identity construction, 2, 5–11, 19–22, 28, 36–7, 165–8
  as luxury, 28
  as tradition, 26–7, 36–7, 166
forgery, 27, 112–14. *See also* art
Freeman, Morgan, 102

GATs (genetic ancestry testing), 145–7, 150, 152, 164, 171.
  See also ancestry; biological essentialism
gender
  constructions of, 51, 96, 149, 156–7
  as feminine, 89, 156–7
  gender bias, 51–3
  as identity, 156, 159, 161
  (in)equity, 51–3, 141–2
  power-dynamics, 51–3, 54, 66, 74, 127–9, 157
  transgender, 154, 157, 161
genuine. *See under* authenticity
George IV (king), 170–1
Gilmore, Ruth Wilson, 64
Giménez, Cecila, 112

globalization, 5–6, 11, 30, 45–6, 48
Glossolalia, 118, 120–2
grape leaves. *See dolmas*
Greece
  Athens, 16, 19, 22
  Greek food, 16, 164
  Greek myths, 103–4
  as identity, 19–22
  Thessaloniki, 16–19, 22
Greek salad, 16–22
Greenaway, Roger, 7–8

haggis, 165–6, 175
Hale, Tom, 144
Headley, Walter, 100
Henderson, Bobby, 131
Herapocrypha, 35–7
Highland Society of London, 169, 171
history
  claims of historical authenticity, 12, 96, 113, 156, 165, 172–3
  as contested, 17, 97–100, 168–9
  as constructed narrative, 49, 52, 73–4, 80, 90, 96, 103–4, 125–6, 137, 156–7, 161, 167, 170, 172–3
  as contested, 17, 97–100, 168–9
  claims of historical authenticity, 12, 96, 113, 156, 165, 172–3
  as modern project, 1, 3, 12, 75, 89, 96, 102–5, 110, 151, 155, 161, 165, 169, 173–4
  whitewashing of, 152
  See also anachronism; narrative construction; tradition
Homer, 103
Hory, Elmyr de, 114
Hughes, Aaron W., 6, 40

ideology, 2, 42–3, 47, 74–6, 146,
    154–5
  American political ideology, 140
  neuronormative ideology, 119–21
identification, operational acts of,
    ix–x, 10–11, 40–1, 43, 47, 142,
    156, 164, 166, 169–70
  boundary policing of, 60, 155–6
    160–1, 166
  self-identification, 39, 42, 88–9,
    93–4, 126, 154–7
  as strategic, x, 20, 65, 83, 87, 90,
    92, 160–1
identity
  as ancestry/heritage. *See* ancestry
  as appearance/beauty, 51–3
  as biological, 144–7, 151, 157
  as class identity, 2, 38, 45, 47–8,
    66, 157, 169
  and commodity, 11, 40, 42, 49
  as contested, 12, 93–4, 118,
    128–9, 133–4, 155, 160
  as difference-making, 127–8,
    136, 156–7, 161
  as food, 5–6, 19–22, 30–2, 165–6
  as gendered. *See* gender
  as imagined community, 9, 42, 80
  as individual. *See* individual
  as marginalized, 127–8, 139–40,
    142, 146, 150, 157, 159, 169
  as nationality, 5–6, 19, 165,
    167–8
  as queer, 149, 152, 157, 161
  as racialized. *See* ethnicity; race;
    racism
  as religious, 83–5, 93, 118, 121,
    125–6, 133
inauthenticity, claims of, 1, 6, 10,
    12, 18–19, 24, 27, 30–1, 41,
    63, 65, 93, 97, 109–10, 118–20,
    135–8

as fake, 1, 4, 6, 10–11, 19, 23, 28,
    65, 114–15
incels, 87–90
  KTHHV, 87–8, 90
  vs. orbiters, 88
Incels.co, 87, 89–90
Inception (film), 41
Indigeneity
  and ancestry, 144–7
  heritage and erasure of, 150
  as identity, 76, 149
  Indigenous peoples, 67, 71, 75–6,
    97, 99
  Indigenous resistance, 67
  marginalization and domination
    of, 66–7, 74
  narratives, 73, 75
  See also appropriation; colonial-
    ism; ethnicity; race; racism
Indigenous Peoples March, 74
individual
  as autonomous, 40–2, 65, 76, 79
  as constructed, 79–80, 93
  as consumer, 40, 48
  as distinct, 8–9, 21, 40, 72, 79,
    145
  as inner self, 4, 39, 42, 136, 156.
    See also self-help books
  tyranny of individualism, 65, 72,
    74–6, 79–80, 98, 164
insider/outsider. *See* us vs. them
Intelligent Design, 131
Internal Revenue Service (IRS), 132
Irn-Bru, 165–8, 175
Irving, Clifford, 115
Islam
  as classification, 139–40, 161
  Prophet Muhammad, 161
  Sunnah, 159, 161
  See also Muslims
Islamophobia, 80–1, 139–40

184 *Fabricating Authenticity*

Italy, 2–3, 7, 10
  Italian food, 3, 10, 21, 25–6, 30, 36
  King Umberto I and Queen Margherita, 25
  Kingdom of Italy, 25–6

James IV and I (king), 172
James, Esther A. et al., 51
Jay-Z (Shawn Carter), 61
Jediism. *See* Temple of the Jedi Order (TOTJO)
Jenner, Caitlyn, 154–7
jewels, 46–9
Johnson, Josh, 108–10
Judaism, 107–8, 127–9, 134
  as identity, 159

Kansas, 159
  Kansas City BBQ, 5
  Kansas School Board, 131
  Karhun kansa (People of the Bear), 137
Kates, Naama, 89–90
Katz, Nathan, 127–9
kilt, 168–70, 172
Kim, Gene, 121
Klein, Naomi, 84–5
Krug, Jessica A., 159–60, 162

La Sazón de Mexico, 30–1
label. *See* classification
Lakota Sioux Nation, 75, 97, 99.
  See also Indigeneity; *Ťhuŋkášila Šákpe* (Six Grandfathers)
language, 20, 73, 149
  etymology, 1, 17–19, 168–9
  as meaning-making, 47–8, 96–7
Laycock, Joseph P., 132
legitimation processes, x, 2, 5–7, 10, 12, 23, 31–2, 35, 63–4, 66,
  93, 99, 100, 108, 118–20, 122, 133, 137, 140–2
Lincoln, Bruce, 170
luxury
  category of, 46, 48–9
  definitions of, 46–7, 49
  as language or system of meanings, 42, 48–9
  See also commodity; consumerism

MacDonald, Peter, 172–4
Mad Men (TV show), 7, 39, 41
MAGA (Make America Great Again), 71, 73–4.
makeup, power dynamics of, 51–3.
  See also gender
Mamdani, Mahmood, 139–40
marketing
  as branding, 2, 9, 31, 39, 48–9, 84–5, 137, 140–1, 167, 170
  as logo, 31, 84–5
  See also advertisement
Martin, Craig, 132–3
Marx, Karl, 40, 48
Masuzawa, Tomoko, 107
McCann Erickson, 7. *See also* Coca-Cola
McCutcheon, Russell T., x, 6, 24–5, 28, 84, 121, 145, 171
meaning-making, x, 1, 13, 23–4, 27, 47–9, 63, 72–3, 79, 88–9, 92–3, 96–7, 102–5, 110, 142, 145, 164, 166, 174
media
  authorized media objects, 117–22
  fake news, 74, 76
  new media objects, 119
  news media, 60, 64–5, 71–6, 79, 81, 92, 97–100, 108–9, 132, 173

Index 185

See also advertisement; social media
memory, 36–7
Mexico
  Mexican food, 5–6, 30–2, 36, 38
  as identity or heritage, 6, 30, 151–2
  U.S.-Mexico border, 80–1, 149, 151
Minassian, Alek, 87
misogyny, 87–90
  women as femoid or foid, 89–90
Mona Lisa, 27
Moonies. *See* World Peace and Unification Sanctuary
Morris, Meaghan, 45
Mother Mary, 113–15
Mount Rushmore. *See Tȟuŋkášila Šákpe* (Six Grandfathers)
Muslims, 80–1, 139–40, 162
  as authentic, 160–2
  as category, 161
  trans* Muslims, 159–62
  as visible, 140

NAACP (National Association for the Advancement of Colored People), 154–5
Nahuatl, 149. *See also* Indigeneity
naming. *See* classification
narrative construction, x, 3, 10, 12, 57, 73, 75, 81, 92, 96, 100, 160, 175
  as competing, 73–4, 166
  historical narrative, 172–3
  as identity, 10–11, 139–40, 165, 167–8, 172
  as indigenous-centered, 75
  origins narrative, 1, 7, 9–10, 18, 21, 23, 24–7, 102, 117, 127, 137, 166–8, 171–2

  as strategic, 32, 74, 80–1, 114, 139–40, 156, 172
  victim narrative, 74, 76, 81
nationalism
  American, 79–80, 97–100
  as constructed, 96
  symbolic nationalization, 65
  white nationalism, 144
Native American. *See* Indigeneity
Neo-Nazi, 92, 144, 146
nepantla, 149–50, 152
New Seekers, The, 7–8
Newton, Richard, 63–4
Nike, 84–5. *See also* marketing
No Logo (Klein), 84
Nolan, Christopher, 41
Nongbri, Brent, 102
Northern Cheyenne Tribe, 75. *See also* Indigeneity

O Brother, Where Art Thou? (film), 102–4
Odyssey (Homer), 103–5
Omaha Tribe, 71. *See also* Indigeneity
origins. *See under* narrative construction
Osterweil, Vicky, 65–6
Outback Steakhouse, 5
Outlander (TV series), 169

Pals, Daniel, 128–9
Panofsky, Aaron, and Joan Donovan, 145
past, the. *See* history
Pastafarianism. *See* Church of the Flying Spaghetti Monster
Peltier, Leonard, 75
performativity, 21, 37, 48, 117–22, 156, 164
petro-state, 64–8

186 *Fabricating Authenticity*

philanthropy. *See* charity
Phillips, Nathan, 71–6
Phillips, Whitney, 73
pizza, 25–6, 30, 36
Potato Jesus, 112
power dynamics, 1–2, 38, 42, 45–7,
51–3, 66–8, 74–5, 80, 90, 94, 98,
127–9, 132–3, 140–2, 152, 157,
160–1, 169–70
Prince, 61
private vs. public, x, 4–6, 9, 11–12,
31, 60, 64, 74, 79–80, 84–5, 98,
127, 132, 135–6, 139–40, 150,
156
Prothero, Stephen, 125–6, 129

QAnon, 81

race
as essentialized/stereotyped, 88,
145–7, 151, 154, 156–7
as identity, 150, 155, 159
material conditions of, 64, 66–7
race-making, 66, 96, 128, 162
racial justice, 97
transracial, 154–6, 159
See also biological essentialism
racism, 75, 85, 93, 151
as hate speech, 73
racial purity, 144–6
systemic racism, 64, 66–7, 74,
97–100, 140, 146–7, 160
as white supremacy, 64, 144–6,
151, 154, 160
See also capitalism, colonialism
Ramey, Steven, x, 96
Rational Choice Theory, 41
Rawlinson, Thomas, 169–70
Red Pill/Black Pill, 88–90
Reed, Adolph, Jr., 154

religion, category of, 40, 43, 96,
102, 104, 118, 127–8, 132–3,
135, 137–8
as authentic/real, 37, 117,
119–20, 133, 139
as inauthentic, 84, 108–9, 118,
138, 139
as legally recognized, 127, 132,
135–7, 139
non-religion, 43, 128
as satire or parody, 132–3, 135–6
as unique, 138
religion, definitions of, 96, 107–8,
132–3, 135–6, 142
power dynamics of, 128–9, 132–3
Religious Education (RE), 107–8
religious experience, 84, 119–21
religious freedom, 127–9, 132
religious studies as academic discipline, 40, 43, 96, 102–5, 107–8,
110, 121, 125–9, 142
world religions, 107, 137
See also scholarship
Republican National Convention
(RNC), 75–6, 81
restoration
art restoration, 104, 112–15,
117–18
building restoration, 102, 165
See also art
ritual, 80, 89, 92, 117–18, 121,
136–7
ritual attention, 119–20
ritual performance, 120–1
as sacred, 119
Robinson, Cedric, 67
Rodger, Elliot, 87
Rogan, Joe, 71–2, 74
Rogers, Everett M., 39
Roof, Dylann, 154

Index 187

Sandmann, Nicholas, 75–6, 79, 81
Satanic Temple (TST), 132
scholarship
 as description or essentialization, 93, 103–4, 126–9
 as meaning-making, 63, 93–4, 102–5, 107, 110, 129, 142
Scotland
 Edinburgh, 39, 164–5, 168, 170
 Glasgow, 167–8
 as identity/heritage, 165–75
Scott, Sir Walter, 170–1
Scottish Tartan Authority, 172–3
self-help books, 4–5, 175
Sheedy, Matt, 79–81
Shirley, Susan, 8–9
signifiers. *See* symbols
Sikhism, 139–42
Simmons, K. Merinda, 160
Smith, Jonathan Z., x, 5–6, 114, 121
Smith, Leslie Dorrough, 89
Smith, Martha, 92, 150–1
social media, 24, 31, 75–6, 81, 92, 118–19, 140
 trolls, 73
 See also media
Songvisava, Bo, 24–5
Southern Poverty Law Center (SPLC), 80, 93
Spain, 112, 150
Star Wars (films), 137
Stone, Perry, 118–21
Sugar Skull Cantina, 31
Sullivan, Winnifred Fallers, 127–9
symbols
 boundary formation, 46–7, 74–5, 80, 170
 as identity, 48, 168–9
 as strategic, 2, 10, 49, 65, 72–6, 79–81, 85, 90

Taco Boyz, 31
tacos, 5–6, 30–2, 36, 38
Taira, Teemu, 136, 139, 142
tartan, 168–75
 Glen Affric tartan, 172–3
Temple of the Jedi Order (TOTJO), 135–8, 139
terrorism, 80–1, 99–100, 139–40
Thailand
 Thai Buddhist monks, 108–10
 Thai food, 24–5, 30
The Repair Shop (TV series), 113
Theweleit, Klaus, 90
They Live (film), 42
Tȟuŋkášila Šákpe (Six Grandfathers), 97, 99
Touna, Martha, 18, 21–2
Touna, Vaia, 12, 16–20, 22, 107, 109
tradition
 as authentic, 8, 10, 24, 31–2, 109, 129
 definitions of, 127, 129, 132–3, 142
 as high tradition vs. little tradition, 127–9
 and identity, 125, 142, 166, 173
 invention of, 26–7, 169–71
 as meaning-making, 142, 166, 174
 as norm or standard, 96, 125–9
 as uninterrupted, 137, 172–3
 See also memory; narrative construction, origins narratives
trans
 as identity, 154–7, 160–2
 trans* Muslims, 159–62
 transgender, 154, 157, 161
 transracial, 154–6, 159
Trendy Singh, 141–2
Trevor-Roper, Hugh, 169–71

188 *Fabricating Authenticity*

Trump, Donald, 74–6, 80–1, 97–100
  as baby Christian, 83–5
  and locker room talk, 83
  Presidential campaign, 71, 76
  See also MAGA (Make America Great Again)

Uddin, Asma T., 132
Ugly Delicious (TV series), 34–7
UN (United Nations), 66
United States
  Christian hegemony of, 92, 125, 140
  as identity, 6, 140, 144, 147, 151, 167
  nationalism, 79–80, 97–100
  post 9/11, 139–40
  systemic racism, 98–100, 144, 146
  U.S.-Mexico border, 80–1, 149, 151
university, 19, 55–8, 65, 102, 126, 145
us vs. them
  as insider vs. outsider, 32, 36, 65, 75, 108–9, 110, 121, 127–8, 136, 139–40, 146
  as self vs. other, 6, 11–12, 25, 39, 42, 52, 90

  as primitive or savage, 11, 166, 169–70

value
  as commodity, 40, 48–9, 114
  as constructed, 25, 40, 43, 48, 53, 54, 115, 139–40, 152
  Sikh values of equity, 141–2
  as *sui generis*, 40
  values voters, 83
Vatican, the, 126, 133
Veblen, Thorstein, 47, 49
veganism, 30
vegetarianism, 2, 30
Victoria, Queen, 171
Vogue (magazine), 42, 157

Walsh, Joan, 156
Warhol, Andy, 10–11
wastelanding, 66
Welles, Orson, 114–15
Weiss, Bari, 71–2, 74, 76
Wolf, Eric, 1–2
World Peace and Unification Sanctuary, 93
Wounded Knee Massacre, 75

Zhang, Jenny, 35
Zhang, Sarah, 144, 146–7
Žižek, Slavoj, 42